ELEVATED MIND -

Nuggets for Victorious Living.

AKOGWU ELAIGWU

ELEVATED MIND -Nuggets for Victorious Living.

Akogwu Elaigwu

ISBN:

13: 9781722611002

10: 1722611006

INTEGRATED METHODOLOGIES

www.integratedmethodologies.com

method@integratedmethodologies.com

dodgetheiceberg543@gmail.com

Also, check for ''Miraculous Music for Miracles '' at
CreateSpace Amazon

Printed in USA.

Also, check for ''Miraculous Music for Miracles '' at
CreateSpace Amazon

TOPICS

A

‘’...It is also good to look at the-big-picture, and think out-of-the-box...’’

-   Anita Kamal

''...There is no Witch, but the bitter Covet; who, his talents had buried, and no Witchcraft, but Covetousness...''

- Akogwu Elaigwu

B

STATEMENT

''Beloved, I pray that you may PROSPER IN ALL THINGS and BE IN HEALTH, just as your Soul PROSPERS''
3 John 3

C

With Glory to God Almighty, Most High, The Possessor and Maker of Heaven and Earth; God of All Flesh. Benedictions to His Name.
Praised be He.

D

i

ACKNOWLEDGEMENT

All Scriptural Quotations are taken from The STUDENT BIBLE, unless otherwise stated or paraphrased.

D

ii

GRATITUDE

Much gratitude go to all those who have contributed remotely or tangibly to bringing forth this book, and to many, who may not have been mentioned but, who still have equal gratitude; immense gratitude to my Parents, Brothers and Sisters; to my eldest Brother, Daniel E.; then, including Anita Indi Joseph, sponsor of my scholarship; to St. John Bosco Scholarship Scheme; to St. Patrick's Old Boys Association; to J. Bocco; also, regards to J. Oswald Sanders; Zack Moshe; Eli B.; Eli Levit; Kayode L; Agbani F.; Amnon C.; R. Etido; Inalegwu P.; Fidelis O.; Shade Olu; Olohi P; Musa T.; Bamidele S.;

T. Ude Emeka; T. Ekpe; Patricia Oluwaseun; Hyacinth O; R, Moughalu; The Okpanehes; the Adokas; and also, close to the Pavilion, Joy S.; Miss Victoria Elaigwu.

E

INTRODUCTION

A debate on the rising quotient of Freezing of the Intellect, leading to the multiplicity of Locked Minds Congregants, caused by dogmatic spiritism and religionism.

The persistent and prevalent case of supernaturalismic expectationism, may impede the Youths from taking their place in the twenty second century, especially, as regards the practicality to meet the demands and needs of Life. With intense scrutiny, one can see the creeping in not-liking-work mien, as everyone seems want fast miracles. There is gathering fear of the cataclysmic effect of another dark age, void of Intellect, taken over by spiritistism, churchianism, and religionismic faithism* and believism.

*Yet, God Almighty could still be Worshipped without the suffocation of spiritism and religionism.

And this, in no way refer to, nor castigate any organized   religion (s) or religious structure (s), but the dogmatism that is breeding a seemingly exhilarating supernaturalismic expectationism, that may then, later, turn bizarre.

For, after everyone has gone for supernaturalismic expectationism, there will be no one left in the Farm, and the third horse Rider of the Apocalypse may ride in, even before his time. Apart from that, the multiplicity of congregants with Locked Minds, sans Intellect-Liberty, - without Universal Peoplehood Intellectual Nimbleness, is a type of '' Tower-of-Babel'' Togetherism, by which any act of terrorism is possible, with the enchantment of Martyrdom Complex, Suicidism and, worse, the Tribicides that the misanthropy of it could engender.

Therefore, the proffering of the concept of Econo-Industrial Theology as foundation for religions, and/or religious study is the way forward, to avoid the cataclysm.

E

ii

INTRODUCTION

   The use of the Scriptures is for the Physical and Spiritual purposes. A Person, who has Spiritual Disorder, may not expect to have a good Standard of Living.
The very Spiritual Activities are the Physical Work done to make and maintain a Living, because the Flesh-Body, is the Sanctuary of the Spirit. Maltreating the body affects the spirit. People are not alive on Earth to become ''spirits'' all over again, but, to ''physicalize'' and manifest Spirit Essence,

through physical productiveness, constructiveness and creativity. John 17:15

The Parable of Jesus, are very much for the betterment, improvement and prosperity of the Physical Life and Physical Welfare.

The Kingdom Life, which is the Edenic Life, is the Life of living in prosperity and worshiping God Almighty. One can not worship God Almighty three times a day, without having Divine Inspiration, leading to Practical Wisdom, which will bring about Constructive Activity for Prosperous Living.

The Parables are for ''Kingdom Life'' Prosperity on Earth, which prosperity, is about worked-for, earned and deserved wealth that gives to charity, and joyful productive progress, stage by stage, while worshiping God Almighty.

The Edenic Life, being the originally intended life or Living Standard, must be returned to, if, at all, Man actually gained Salvation and Redemption.

Claiming, to have Redemption and Salvation, without having even a semblance of the Edenic Life, as intended from the beginning is bizarre.

Work and the Daily Activities for Living and Making a Living, is the first law of Eden; for, in the beginning, God Almighty, Himself, set about to the Creation Construction Site or Work Place, whereat, He Worked seriously to banish primeval and primordial poverties (emptiness, void, darkness, formlessness, nothingness, nudity, homelessness, etc.) Genesis 1:1; and when He created Adam, God, Himself, being the First Farmer and Gardener, put and taught Man to do such Work, likewise. Genesis 2:8.

The conception of a Paradise or Eden, as a state, condition or situation of ''no work'', or ''worklessness'' and/or, the perception of Work as a curse, is faulty, and a very misleading notion of the sloth. Absence of work is no enjoyment, as in refuting responsibilities to seek ''luck.'' To conceptualize a heaven, where there will be no work, is the imagination of the sloth. He, who offers to Man Salvation or Redemption, without Work on his (the Man's) part, even to exert himself mentally, thereby, has deluded and impoverished him, nay, destroyed him! No one alive, be he of the proletariat, bourgeoisie or aristocrat, or not, has been totally able to escape Work; for everyone must, at least, engage in Mental Labour to have a Living, and Mental Labour, is in itself, a ''headaching'' Work.

The Physical and Practical Work, which Men do on Earth, is the Actual Spiritual Activity, and such Work, in which they exert themselves in, mentally or physically, is the tacit and vivid expression of their gratitude for life and their thankfulness and appreciation to Almighty God, the Creator and Maker of Heavens and the Worlds.

The Original Work of Adam was to dress the Earth, tend it and keep it.   Genesis 2:15. For, lo, the Earth is one big Garden- Man, therefore, is a Constructive Promoter and Worker in/of Creation, by his Activities on Earth, which must never be destructive, but totally and explicitly constructive.

To ignore the Earth, Earthlife, and the Creative and Industrious Activities of It, in an ''utopic'' quest, or involvement in supernaturalismic expectionism, is a grave indifference, which is destructive. For, we hear that: ''God s-o-o-o-o-o-o Love the Earth, and He gave...''; and why would not God Almighty love His own Creation? Why then, must a Man live in abstraction to the Earth and Earthlife, and fail to Work Constructively in it?

Man, by the Physical and Practical Work and Labour, which he does on Earth, offers expiation for his own iniquities too, in part; for the Redemption of Man is wrapped up in his labour, inclusive of the labour for his Livelihood, which labour, is constructive towards the Creative Deific Will, Fiat. Hence, Constructive Work is the actual Atonement for Man, as such constructive work lead to the global peace missions, universal peoplehood, inventions to ease living, missions for liberty, missions for human rights, charities (of which, without charities, the salvation is mere noise), etc.

No success without sweat, sweat managed for the

profit, and for the labour of transubstantiation of the Earth and service to Humanity, for the Edenic Life. Spiritual nimbleness or Faith* without applicable physical exertion yields nothing.

*Faith has become ''work cubed'', (F=W3), that is, Work raised to the third power or degree.

When God Almighty said: ''Let there be'', The Elohimic Spirit- Energies (Doing Rhema), moved (worked), and ''There was''(Things were made); for, lo, The Logos (Word) worked with the Rhema (Spirits), were Elohims (God's Spirit Beings, Elohims, Angels, Begotten, Rhema, etc. and of the Cherubs and Seraphs of the Circle-Seven; they are the ''Spirit Elohimic Workers'', of which we hear, ''Let 'Us' make'', the ''elohim-us-gods'', ...as ''The Spirit hovers above the Waters''; and, lo, ''hovering'' is Big inspectorate Work; therefore, God sweated to make and create, which is why as you can observe in Nature, nothing is allowed to waste, because He laboured to make every seemingly tiny thing, so that, even what is putrefied, becomes manure and yield more life-forms. Does the giant excavator has more living brain than the seemingly tiny Ant? Even so, is Man a seemingly tiny speck when compared to Behemoth, which was the First of God's Way in Creation. Therefore, God went on a Sabbatical Leave well deserved, after His Labour, of which there would have been no need, if He had not worked, and every time we look about, we see and feel the great work of God Most High, and the more reason an ungrateful sloth and vandal will have nothing in it.

God Almighty makes, and gives to Man to make, for the Edenic Life and Living- to Become and Be, as it ought to be from ''the beginning''.Anything which is malevolent, misanthropic, destructive, which ''beareth not fruit'' that prospers, promotes, supports Creation and the Edenic Life, will be hewed down and spewed away.

The pursuit of Righteousness,* brings Prosperity naturally, especially when One adopts Spiritual Intelligence, to stay defended against the Evil Cohorts.

*Righteousness, in this context means: Doing the Right Things to live well with Initiative, but not religiosity), is invariably and obliquely, the pursuit of prosperity.

A Man can not live righteously and fail to prosper, for, the expressions of the prosperity laws are the actual laws of righteousness. People who say that they live righteously, but fail to prosper, may actually and realistically, not have been DOING THE RIGHT THINGS.

The True Riches of ''The Kingdom'', come through Work and a Character of Righteousness, by the Kingdom Blessedness in this very Life on Earth. And true prosperity is noted- DOING THE RIGHT THINGS.

The Life of Righteousness* manifested as Excellent Reputation constitute Personality Recommendation that promotes.

*Righteousness in this parlance means Excellent Reputation

It is the Excellent Reputation that keeps One in tune with Kingdom Blessedness, and that is what the Enemies and

bitter Covets are after, to demolish his Reputation, and once they demolish the Person's Excellent Reputation (Righteous Character) or the Person demolishes it by himself, he leaves the laws of prosperity, and fails.

This, for the Tranquility of Life,

That, Man may see the True Light,

That Man may Live in The Peace,

To see that the benefit of Life, is the possible Happiness and Liberty,

That Wisdom leads Man to Creativity and the Worship of God Almighty (Glory to His Name).

F

PROLOGUE

Divine Inspiration received and acted upon, is the high road to victory and prosperity in Life and Living*

*It is one thing to have Life, and another thing to Make an excellent Living.

For, by such Divine Inspiration, comes creativity, inventiveness, constructiveness, industriousness, enterprise, trade, art, etc.

The most practically and physically active, is the most spiritual. Spirit is active verve, not insipidity.

The relevance of Divine Inspiration/Idea is manifested in the ''Physicalization'', materialization industrialization, actualization, of the hitherto Spiritual Energies and Verve, through Creative Work on the Earth Plane. Spiritual nimbleness or engagement without Material Relevance to the Earth and Earth-Living is null spiritism.

Therefore, those who, in religious frenzy, dogmatism, fanaticism, bigotry, etc., try to abdicate or remove themselves from matter/materials are wrong, because, even the very air we breathe is gaseous and gas is matter. Man must adjust to adapt to the Realities of Nature and Material Existence; he, being in a World of Matter, as to avoid abuses and adjust to, and use matter as long as he is on Earth.

G

PREFACE

The Parables of ''The Kingdom'',
illustrate the   should-be Kingdom Life,
which signify that the Kingdom Life is a
Life of Happiness, Liberty and Prosperity.

Hidden in the Parables are nuggets
for the physical and spiritual prosperity as
of the should-be Kingdom Life, which
typifies or is the prototype of the actual
Life of Paradise, which ''is to come'', in
the ''Fullness of Time'', when the Earth
becomes the New Earth, or is Edenized to
be, as it was supposed to be.

Then, the Parables of The Kingdom,
shall become real; but, even now, those
who can dig into them, can, of
themselves, set themselves to live happily,

in liberty, and prosperity, through understanding of the Hidden Wisdom, nay, of the Blessedness of having the Aura and Essence of the Almighty God.

Use your TALENT, like the FIVE WISE VIRGINS, so as to invest your MUSTARD SEED, with the skill of WATCHFULL SERVICE, as do responsible WORKERS IN THE VINEYARD, who cultivated the GROWING SEED, having and using the knowledge of the HIDDEN TREASURE AND PEARL OF GREAT VALUE.

H

TALENT

Matthew 25:14-30

Men received properties, wages, things, talents, gifts, inheritance, money, salaries, contracts, opportunities, chances, time, etc.

NUGGET LINE:

''The Man who had received Five Talents, went at once and put his money to work and gained five more''

Matthew 25:16

NUGGET POINT:

''For everyone who has, will be given more, and he will have an abundance''
Matthew 5:29

INFERENCE:

The merchandise of the Merchant is profitable and beneficial no matter how small.

The One who ''has'' to whom ''more is given'' is the One who makes profit by trading, investing, working with what he has been given whether small or big.

He ''has'', because, he MAKES PROFITS, by putting to work what he receives, whether what he receives is big or small. Only he who works with, invests to increase profit is said to have; the profit he makes, is the ''more given'' to him; for, he who does not make profits, lacks the securities to continue to be relevant, hence, diminishes.

ASSIGNMENT:

Go at once and put your Talent (monies, skills, resources, inheritance, gift, etc.) TO WORK, by trading, marketing, saving, investing, -working on it or putting it to work to render payable, profitable services to maximize profit or gains – promptly meeting needs.

Learn not to depend on the Future nor on that which is not yet; that is a mistake a lot of people do, when they talk of ''believing'' as the criteria to meet needs and ignore the practical activity by which to get what they need, and rather chose to depend on hopes, expectations, promises, etc., which are not yet. Think of it, how could a person be so callous to depend on expectations or hope, which he ought to, rather be working on? Even the Devils believe, but their belief is of no significance because it lacks positive actions in the proximity and line of same such belief of theirs. Faith or Belief is not the main criteria, because God will be God and do what he likes to do, whether a Man believes or not. Most miracles were done to people who did not even believe a dot; and as if, their unbelief became catalysts to explore, which made them got answers; and more to that, when you consider that most faiths or beliefs were presumption, fear of hell or docility/gullibility. What percentage of Faith did the Semites in the Exodus have? Even their Leader doubted from day one. Yet, nowhere else in the Scripture have we seen the greatest miracles, than done to those unbelieving migrants. Faith or Belief may just have been used as an apologetic or excuse as to why a miracle did not happen, in order to massage the egos of the preachers and to retain the number of congregation. Can you see how far they go to accuse people of ''lacking faith''. Ask: Would she have come there, if, she did not believe? If a Miracle* did not happen, it just did not, therefore just go more practical and physical, wisely. And God may not answer all prayers; He can not be commandeered.

> *What brings Miracles most, is not mere belief/faith, but Attunement to the Aura and Essence of God Almighty to receive Divine Inspiration/Idea and the ability to work on the idea.

What Jesus meant by ''Faith'', is not what many people today call it. Many people today just want quick fixes, without the labour of mental calculations, and the more reason, the preachers sweet-talk them. What Jesus meant by ''Faith'', was Spiritual Attunement to the Aura and Essence of God Most High, attained by

Spiritual Intelligence, that result to Physical Motion/Activity. This does not repudiate faith or belief, but to know how to apply your faith and belief to you practical work and to yourself. It is even better to worship One's self, than to worship Idols.

Therefore, Wisdom always stands apart to lead you to USE your talent to profit, to be given more, as that profit. More is just profit accruable from investment or trade, meaning that, the One who has, may not have more added to him, if, he did not invest or cultivate, what he has. One's future is tied to what he is doing now or does now, or the works of now in totality.

The availability of Charity or Divine Providence can not condone slothfulness nor does Charity relinquish or take away One's Responsibilities, Duties, Obligations or Self-Care, not even in Heaven; for, God, Himself, hitherto worketh. God may not help a Man beyond his Responsibilities.

I

TEN VIRGINS

People set about for their livelihood.

NUGGET LINE:

''The Wise, however, TOOK OIL JARS ALONG WITH THEIR LAMPS'' Matthew 25:4

NUGGET POINT:

''Therefore, keep watch, because you do not know the day nor the hour''

INFERENCE:

They prepared and equipped, took the fortune, keep thriving.

Real Faith is Wisdom in Action and Wisdom involves Foresight Action to PLAN AHEAD, by SAVING money or resources for One's needs. One can not depend on ''expectation'', because, no one knows the day adversity or want may come. PREPARATION, tangible, substantial, mental preparation for the needs, is what faith is. Note that, no one can be totally and fully prepared, which is why for a person not to even have any preparation logistic at all, makes the mountain fall on him. Many peoples' problems were avoidable, but it was just that, they did not even have up to 50% preparation in relation to PLANING AHEAD. It is not smart for One not to know what he may need, and prepare regularly, substantially, mentally, financially, or otherwise for it. Some People had sacrificed and wasted huge bulls and monies on the Altar of Spiritisc Ritualism, the very Sum that could have been their Pension in Life, which could have salvaged them in Old Age.

ASSIGNMENT

   Take EXTRA Oil in Jars along. That is, by extension, keep your financial account balance green. And, NEVER allow yourself to Lack Basic Needs and Necessities of Life and of Making a Living; because, Basic Needs of Life ensures One's Liberty and Happiness, which keeps One away from servitude, witches, manipulation, seduction, swindlers, slavery, dependency, hell, etc.,(LEARN TO EQUIP AND PREPARE FOR THE OPPOSITE OF YOUR PRESENT SITUATION)

        The prosperity, happiness and liberty obtained from Practical Wisdom, give One the arena to Worship God Almighty, using his FORESIGHT, in a preventive and solution oriented action. Knowing that something may be needed and being financially ready is the Wisdom of the Five ''Wise Virgins'', which lets them into the Banquet of the Bridegroom''

Has One ever asked: Why this particular Five Virgins took extra oil in jars along with them when they were going to meet the ''ALMIGHTY'' Bridegroom? When One answers this question aright, he begins to pity the situation of today's high level Spiritual Dependency, and the exploitation by Spiritism and religionism on them; and finally finds that those Five Wise Virgins, may even have been wiser than stated, because, perhaps, 1 out of 10, in ordinary life situation, may have bothered carrying extra oil in jars going, not merely to meet, but to the [Real-LIVE Banquet], of which they were invitees, of the supposedly ''almighty'' Bridegroom, and that ''1'', may be relative to the Bridegroom or organizers. How many people in thousands, carry extra oil in jars going to Wedding Banquets in ordinary life? This is just to show the extent of personal responsibilities and preparedness, that this Parables, does not merely speak of ceremonial event banquets.

Again One could ask: Where is the altruism of socialism that we all talk about? No altruistic lean-on-me, dependency or   chain-begging here. The other ''Five'' that did not carry extra oil in jars along with them, lacked oil thereafter, and begged, but were not given. Which may show the fakery of altruism, destructive togetherism, communism , socialism, unionism, expectationism, etc., when personal responsibilities are ignored.

J

SHREWD MANAGER

A Manager is asked to give account of his Management.

NUGGET LINE:

''Whoever can be trusted with very little can also be trusted with much, and whoever is dishonest with little, will also be dishonest with much''

NUGGET POINT:

''For the people of this world, are more shrewd in dealing with their own kind...So, if you have not been trustworthy in handling worldly wealth, who will trust you with true riches?''

INFERENCE:

Shrewdness in business, trade, job, job-market, and discipline for frugal savings, will keep One afloat, even after the job is gone. It is good to plant structures that can be of help in times of most need. One has to be able to use small sums of money. As large as multinationals and huge conglomerates are, they talk in cents and pennies, receive/sell their shares in cents and pennies. This, is to show the value of using small sums of money as little drops to make a sea of wealth, it does not call for miserliness.

It is proper to be clever at understanding and making sound judgment about situations in every day living; for, that is what makes One to have the needed happiness, liberty and prosperity – the wise decisions he makes in every situation, which decisions are feasible and tangible.

Good decision making will make One to be able to Achieve Balance, and be able to worship God, while putting his money to prosperous ends and avoiding swindlers.

One has to be shrewd in business, trade or job, as if, One can be called upon to give detailed account at any time. One could buy shares into other businesses; invest in people; do deeds of charity; cast some bread upon the waters; render profitable services to many people...

One also needs to know when to go leverage; know how to liquidate and restart a fresh line of business; understand newer trends in the economy or market; know how to offer loans and make legal documents of Terms and Condition in the agreement; know how to keep away from debt and how to make contract deals, deeds of properties, oaths of allegiance, ethics of service, how to keep One's word and how to make good auditing report, ledger balances, neat sheet report and inventories; to make and have good money saving account; have something to fall back on as a way of personal ''insurance'' or future income source, when the present job or business fails or when money fails; be prepared and equipped for money failure, adversity, bankruptcy, eviction, etc., by having capital asset, treasures, souvenirs, properties and how to diversify economic interest; avoid being carried away by money and neglecting to worship God Almighty every day, three times a day, for, He gives One the Health and Life, which are the powers to prosper. As One can not know what may befall anytime, one needs to have Spiritual Intelligence, by attuning himself to the Divine Presence.

In fact, the very reason, that One can hardly know what may happen in the future, (even though, he could use statistical data to interpolate, estimate or predict, to reach an analysis), is the more reason, why One must have a necessary measure of preparation, tangible (money, properties or capital assets); virtual (ideas, inspiration, creativity, tact); or a relationship (family members, business mates, partners, shareholders, etc.) as preparatory personal securities or insurances, in the line of ForeSight, over a perceived debilitating problem, by making regular assessments of needs, present and future. This means, a Wise Man, ought always to know his next needs and sources of provision for such needs, well in advance, at least two year before.

One's job, as an employee, is enhanced by what he is saving, achieving, investing, from what he has been paid or earned, because, the main troubles, are outside or after the job.

One has to be very serious on the job. Honesty is expensive, so honest managers are expensive too. One may not seek to assuage or reward his managerial efforts, by embezzling, instead, he should make sure that he is well paid, as he will be honest.

K

PRODIGAL SON

Luke 15:11-31

Some people got their share of the estate or properties; gratuity, pension, pay-off, wages, payments, interest, bonuses, emoluments, allowances, etc.

NUGGET LINE:

''So he divided his properties between them''

NUGGET POINT:

''After he had spent everything, there was severe famine in the whole country and he began to be in need''

INFERENCE:

Frugality which include the avoidance of wastes is the highroad to prosperity –frugal management of what you have whether big or small.

The merchandise of the Merchant is beneficial and profitable, no matter how small it may be.

''Wild living'' and the inability to be thrifty and frugal leads to poverty, severe poverty, lacking access to all the basic needs of Life. Is not better to be frugal and thrifty sometimes than to experience such poverty?

Frugality is the strait and narrow way that leads to prosperity; for, it yields the Principal or capital for investment or attainment of securities for the basic needs, leading to wealth. Only a simpleton takes the basic needs of Life for granted.

Yet, Frugality is not miserliness, maladjustment, maladaptation, meanness, etc.

ASSIGNMENT

One has to come to his senses and redeem himself from his losses and wastes and wastages. No One can prosper, who lacks the discipline to avoid extravagances, impulsiveness, hedonism, narcissism, gambling, cyclic redundant ritualism, purchasing luck, promisism, expectationism, hopism, etc.

A ''Sound Mind'' is needed to prosper. People with Thwarted Minds, Spiritual Disorder, Dogmatism or Gullibility Problem, who can not use their ''good senses'', or Common Sense, find themselves always in the wrong path or swindled. And these failings are caused by Mr. Ignorance. They end up wasting what they have and are easily beguiled or swindled, until they by their own profligacy find themselves in poverty, being unable to meet needs, being in dire want. And how can a person, who is unable to meet the basic needs of life be described as intelligent? The problem is that too many people can not learn until it happens, and they are stranded.

One has to remain within the Aura and Essence of God Almighty to have Divine Inspiration, which will position him to prosper and succeed, keeping him away from the profligate ways of wastefulness and emptiness. God Almighty gives you the Brain-Mind and Health to make Wealth, by that, GOD ALMIGHTY HAS ALREADY PROVIDED, SO, USE YOUR BRAIN.

One problem of the times, is that most preachers preach to fill their pews and do not really care about the adherents' Living, so they interpret the Bible to increase their congregations' number only. They will NEVER tell One the other Side of the Scriptures, of its Physical Application, they serve ''cakes not turned''.

Many people today are lost, looking for what God Almighty [Will Do], any where the enter the preachers keep hammering What God WILL DO. They never care to remember that God Almighty HAS ALREADY DONE. And, by the Gift of A Sound Mind, He has already provided, not to mention the abundance given in Nature. SEEK WITHIN YOU TO FIND WHAT YOU HAVE. It is in you, too. Making positive USE of what you have, and avoiding abuse/misuse, so as to prevent dysfunction, waste, malnutrition, disease, eviction, disorder, miserliness, maladjustment, maladaptation, losses, etc.

The very work which men do on Earth, is the tacit expression of their gratefulness and appreciation to God Almighty for the Joy of Life and to have a Living.

One may not have to allow himself to get swept off by the current wave of supernaturalismic expectatiuonism finding what ''God Will Do'', rather, see and use what you have to set your life in order, no matter how small, it may be, for, with good investment, there will be increase.

L

WISE AND FOOLISH BUILDERS

Matthew 7:24-27;
Luke 6:42-49

People build things.

NUGGET LINE:

''He is like a Man, building a house who dug down deep and laid the Foundation on Rock''

NUGGET POINT:

''And he laid the Foundation on Rock''

INFERENCE

People need to get ''The Logos'' and ''The Rhema'', which is the Embodiment of The WORD

and The SPIRIT of God Most High, which is the ''Christ* Anointing''

* Christ, here means Word and Spirit of God Almighty, of the Realm of The ''Elohimic Voice''.

The Word and Spirit of God Almighty in them, will generate The Spiritual Intelligence to make them remain ever prosperous, because of the ''Spiritual Intelligence'' and ''Excellent Spirit'', of the ''Divine Intelligence'' in them, which

Excellent Spirit, is the emanation of the Aura and Essence of God Almighty.

Who taught the ''Genius''? The Genius just seems to know without being taught, as we can see in many Inventors and Discoverers; this does not really mean that the Genius do not learn or are not actually taught, we refer to their Inventions, which had not existed until they made it or knew how to make it, thereby, bringing about new knowledge, which others have to learn from them or study. From where did they get that knowledge that had not been or made that invention that no One had made before? It is because he has The Spirit of Revelation, which is the ''Excellent Spirit'', as was in Daniel, and is always ten times better because of the Intelligence of Divine Inspiration. He is in the Revelation Mode, and so, his Knowledge is inductive, inspirational, rational, reasonable, pragmatic, practical, etc., as it is [From On High], that is, it is

''Christed*'', even though, because of intellectual pride, he may never admit that it comes from God Almighty, and especially as he is not fashioned as a ''Born Again'' God does not require ''Born Againism'' to impart Blessing or Gifts on people, and God's Gifts are not only for evangelism or religion.

*Christed means to be Imbued with and Attuned to the Word and Spirit of God Almighty.

The Rock is the Testimony, which Testimony, is the Knowledge of Christ*, which Christ is the   WORD plus SPIRIT of God Almighty, that imbues and possesses a Man, so that, he becomes set for DOING GOOD*

* Doing Good, here, does not merely mean religious engagement, but Constructive Activities that benefit Humanity and Nature physically and practically.

Therefore, the real Foundation, that ensures prosperity and success is the

Christ* Foundation, which is the Foundation of the Word + Spirit or Logos + Rhema., from whence all cosmic inspirations, knowledge, revelation and the power of such come from, which is the UNIVERSAL CREATIVE MIND, as of the of CREATION ORACLE REALM OF THE CIRCLE SEVEN, of ''Making To Be'', in the very Realm of the I-AM-THAT-I-AM, and from thence, comes the INSPIRATION for happiness, health, liberty, success and prosperity, and even Scriptural Inspiration, comes from there too.

Therefore, any One can not build, in any wise such a building may be, who has not got the ''Excellent Spirit'' from God Most High, even by the very Inspiration, thus relayed, from the Realm, though, they often deny it was God Almighty's Realm as its Origin.

ASSIGNMENT

Get ATTUNED to the Aura and Essence of God Almighty, to receive INSPIRATIONS (IDEAS), of Divine Wisdom, on Living and Making a Living —of Prospering.

M

MUSTARD SEED

Matthew 13:31-32

The smallest thing which grows to become the largest, giving shade, security, cover, etc.

NUGGET LINE:

''Though the smallest of all your seeds, yet when it grows, it is the largest of the garden plants, and become a tree, so that the birds of the air come and perch in its branches''

NUGGET POINT:

''...Which a Man took and planted in his field...''

INFERENCE

''Faith is the SUBSTANCE of things hoped for, the EVIDENCE of things...'' –St. Paul.

Some people, when they want to explain Faith, just resigns themselves to mere beliefs or hopes; worse, mere beliefs, without any Substance and Evidence to show for it, and without Work, therefore, they have a life of no-preparation, like a Man wanting to travel, but who does not prepare in advance to have the fares and luggage first of all, for that, get stranded, and increases his vulnerability, liability, dependency and insecurity.

What faith is said to be is the Substance which One has got tangibly, for achieving his expectation or hope. It is the Evidence or Result, which One has Physically for what he needs. By extension, it is the currency or other means of exchange One has in hand, to get what One really needs. It also involves One's inherent gifts, talent, character, with which to get what One needs.

Therefore, he who can bestir himself, to have at least ten percent of the total requirements or sum needed to mobilize and start, has the substance, evidence or work, to get what he needs; by extension, your ten percent capital, principal, energy, training, know-how, talent, seed, or idea to begin with, is your Mustard Seed, and it is the Seed Capital or Seed Talent which One can sow, which can grow into a Large Tree (Large Tree, here, means profit, dividend, returns, harvest), that offers you shade, security, private income source, insurance, etc., for you and every One in your care.

This means that, One's Faith, is his Mustard Seed evidence, substance, money, resource, result, principal, etc. The Mustard Seed is One's Ten Percent* Mobilization Logistics, to start or begin any project or venture.

*This means that, as soon as you get Ten Percent of the Total Needed Amount, you can begin anything, because, The Ten Percent Mobilization Resource, is your Faith.

Without being able to even have a starting Ten Percent Resource provided by One for the Project, his Faith is Without Work.

Seek and you will find [what you have]. People may not find what they do not have, or more correctly, people may not find what they do not have a Mustard Seed for, inside them and outside them. To get something people have to sow, put, draw, imbibe or magnetize a microcosm of what they want, inside them and outside them.

People, usually, unconsciously, seek what they have and find it, meaning that, what a Person Seeks and Finds, is what he has the Microcosmic Content*   (* The Microcosmic Content is also referred to as Mustard Seed) of, that pulls and magnetizes him to it, meaning that, people are also what they find and seek, because they have the Mustard Seed (Microcosmic Content) of that which they seek and find inside them, therefore what is left is for them, is to provide another Mustard Seed of that in the Physical, and when he does, he automatically puts himself in the path to easily get it, and the mustard seed, thus presented, is his Faith.

No One gets anything for nothing, he must provide at least, even a link from within himself to get it. This means that, even when somebody likes a person, there is something of/in that person that gets to him or that he is attracted to; he could not have liked the person, if, he had not seen anything in him that he admires; therefore, the person he thinks he likes free of charge, is giving him something virtual, and if that person should just take a step further, and do something physical and practical to his admirer, the mere like may turn to love, and he may even receive help, gift, fortune, etc.

What a lot of people need to catapult them to victory or success is to do something physically practical on their desires, just a Ten Percent Activity on it, and it will then allow the hitherto microcosmic content within to blossom forth, that Ten Percent Activity or Provision is the Mustard Seed to let One to SEEK and FIND.

One's Physical and Practical Actions or Tangible Provision, sparks and ignites the inner virtual microcosmic content inside of him or in the other object(s), to bring his needs. That is why a dull and insipid person, who is not physically and practically active, can not have success, in spite of the height of his spiritual powers and how seemingly gifted or full of potentials or prospects as he seems to be, because he can not ignite them to motion. The point in the Mustard Seed theory is that, a person can turn on the ignition for motion for his project to start, if he, at least, could raise Ten

Percent start-up resource, as a Mustard Seed Faith.

One does not have to wait to get Whole Lump Sum or Total Completeness, before he starts anything, once One has Ten Percent Mobilization Substance, he has got his Mustard Seed, to begin sowing, investing, working, etc.

ASSIGNMENT

One has to sow his Mustard Seed in [His Feld], and wait patiently for it to grow, cultivate it, nurture it and wait patiently for it to bear fruit. And to sow his Mustard Seed by [Himself In His Own Field], else, he may lost it or the swindlers may take it from him. One has to put his Talent to Work and have a Righteous Character.

N

WATCHFUL SERVICE

Luke 12:42-48

To the Family Head, Husbands, Fathers, Mothers, Wives, Personnel Manager, Administration Manager, Chief Executive Officers, Ecclesiastical and Pastoral Overseers, Diplomatic Relation Officers, Next-of-Kin, Inheritors, etc.

NUGGET LINE:

''Who is the Faithful and wise manager, whom the master put in charge of his servants to give them their food allowance at the proper time''

NUGGET POINT:

''From every one who has been given much, much will be demanded and from the one that has been entrusted with much, much will be asked''

INFERENCE

One may never become an entrusted Manager of any business, nor serve in the capacity of Chief Executive Officer in any institution, organization, factory, agency or company, nor serve in any administrative position in any venture, successfully, if, he totally lacks the ability to work along with people amicably, because, in the end, character, personality and reputation are what make the sales or get required results, and the best Manager is the One who has that –the One who knows how to coordinate the people and the people, many of them, like to work with him, because he understands the nitty-gritty of human relationship, interaction, communication, association, diplomacy, cooperation, etc., which means that, he is able to lead the people because he is able to influence them positively, in the direction of company's policies towards greater profits.

There is no way that the Manager can function if, he can not earn the confidence of the majority of people, especially those at the top (or superior majority). He must also earn their respect, else, he can not Captain, and being not able to captain, the Ship will founder.

Also, the Man who is the head of the Family, but can not provide for them, when needed is said to be worst than an infidel. How then can the house prosper, whose head does not know how to organize the people towards the central goal of a higher standard of living, happiness, liberty and prosperity for all; and most significantly, lead them to worship God Almighty, because, in that, he also asserts the sincerity of his influence over them, to bring them to The Peace and Unity needed to achieve the significant purposes. This must in no way alter the secularity of the organization and the liberties of the individual worship systems. The security and liberty of the organization must be maintained, but the common ethics must be driven towards thorough humaneness, tolerance, justice, etc.

ASSIGNMENT

To acquire all the traits and develop the character and attitude which makes it possible for One to relate positively with people, which involves giving much where much, been received and entrusted to One, because ''the much'' given to him, were given because of the vast responsibilities which he has over the people he leads, of which it is demanded of him to ''give back much.''

O

WORKERS IN THE VINEYARD

Matthew 20:1-5

They make agreements, deals, contracts, deeds, titles, etc.

NUGGET LINE:

''He agreed to pay them a denarius for the day, and sent them into the vineyard''

NUGGET POINT:

''Didn't you agree to work for a denarius?''

INFERENCE

People, who fail to make proper agreement, settlement, oath of allegiance, bargains, deals, contracts, vows, etc., get into problems always in business and every other aspect of Life and Living.

Apart from those who refrain from making proper oaths of allegiances or agreements, since they claim that, their religious doctrine forbids them from making oaths or swearing, are those who present themselves so kind, meek and polite, that they would not dare make any oath of allegiance or agreement, so that, they do not appear rude, crude or distrusting, and in the end, they always find themselves in the perils, throes and woes of indiscretion and poor decision making.

Terms and Conditions, always applies, and where One has speculated and found that he can not meet it, he should keep off. Condition of Service, Code of Conduct, Affidavits, Organizational Ethics, Undertaking, Letter of Appointment, Engagement, Certificates, Application, Voucher, Receipts, Ledgers, Balance and Inventory Record, Trade Agreement, Contract Agreement, etc., all apply.

In dealing with people, in order to avoid trespasses, One has to learn to do things according to settlements plan reached by both parties and endeavor to avoid breach of contracts agreements, especially when there was no unavoidable or natural causes. After One had agreed, signed and sealed it, it will become legally binding and One has to abide by it, as to let his yes be yes and no be no as had been signed and attested to. Therefore, if there is any code that baffles One, or may cause him some trouble, he ought not sign till he has confirmed or studied it thoroughly. And, lo, many people in religion have problems in this aspect, as they may have been indoctrinated against oaths making, which then lead to poor agreement making standards and the resulting troubles, not only in business, but in day to day interactions and relationships. They are always interpreted by others as being indifferent in key decision portfolios, as they can not reach conclusions; and they even end up causing fractures in relationship and organizational settings which may not have been, if, they had reached agreements earlier on oaths. Therefore, avoid trustism.

ASSIGNMENT

One has to study the business, job, relationship, contract, or deals documents and agreements very well, before he agrees, signs and seal/stamp. He has to settle all money matters amicably and with best practices and promptness.

One must know the depth or gravity of the penalty or comeuppance of any action or inaction, and prepare and equip himself. One must keep away from avoidable debts as far as possible, and avoid debt settlements problems with any person he deals with, even with seemingly trusting people and very close relatives or close family members.

P

GROWING SEED

Mark 4:26-29

Men cultivate and invest in things.

NUGGET LINE:

''Night and Day, whether he sleeps or gets up, the seed sprouts and grows, though, he does not know how''

NUGGET POINT:

''A man sows seeds on the ground...As soon as the grain is ripe, he puts the sickle to it, because the harvest has come''

INFERENCE

The Kingdom of Heaven on Earth, represents the Will of God Almighty (Blessed be He), on Earth, which means that, it will be as it was made to be from the beginning, as proposed by the Creator, Himself; and that responds to and represents the law of Planting and Harvesting practically. Planting and harvesting is not only agriculturally, but also other ways of planting, like investing, working, trading, creativity, art, construction, etc.

It usually appears that Jesus have been presented and pictured by some, as loathing, disdaining and condemning the Earth and the Life on Earth, and preferring poverty and self-immolation; and this belief has transcended into every sphere of their activities, to such extent, that such people condemn any body who seek to improve on the living condition and raise or upgrade the living standard, as anti-christ and devilish. Such conceptions which exist in many congregational denomination, is proven to many other thinkers as the destructive and bewitching aspects of mysticism that brings on a dark era.

It is not surprising that many adherents of such congregations feel guilty when ever they buy or acquire Material Things that ought to improve Living Conditions. It is with such slavery of the Mind, thwarted mind and spiritual disorder, that quite a lot of people practice their religions, and what a woe for the person not awakened enough to shun such dogmatism.

Yet, when One looks at it ''scrutinizingly'', One finds that, presenting Jesus as a pauper and a person who hates and disproves of the Earth, prosperity on Earth and Earth Life, allow such preachers to continue to enslave their adherents who they call flocks and sheep, putting them in thralldom, both spiritually, mentally and physically. The question which ought to be asked is this: ''If, Jesus really hated the Earth, Earthlife, prosperity on Earth and prefers that everyone should live in self-neglect and   self-immolation, why then, did he pray that: ''...Thy Kingdom come...''   { For the Kingdom to come to Earth }, or ,''...Be done on Earth as it is done in Heaven..''? Also, why did he bother himself healing people, if, he loathed,   hated   and   disdained enjoyment, comfort, happiness, liberty, prosperity, etc.?

        And if Jesus is unconcerned about the politics, government, administration, economy, society, education, trade, commerce, etc., why did he embark on the ''Triumphant Entry'' and at that age that he embarked on the triumphant entry, was he so care-free as not to know that it was a very succinct Political Statement one time too loud?

And adding to that, why did he pay tax, and made such statement as ''Give to Caesar, Caesars' things...''?

Again, if, Jesus loathed ''the good life'', enjoyment, prosperity, pleasure, fun, etc., as he is being presented to be, why did he allow Mary Magdalene to pour oil on him the way she often did it, and not once but many times, pouring him oil and massaging his leg and feet? Can such ''footsie'' and massage come so cheap or to a nobody?

Is chiropody, pedicure and makeover so cheap? And on top of that when a socialite and top society Mary M. from the renown Towers of Magdala does it, and with a perfumed oil costlier than a quarter of Joy Perfume?

And again, if Jesus was all about asceticism, self-flagellation, self immolation, why did they never wait to pluck corn when other Shemites thought was proper? Why did he not wait for the fig tree to reach fruition time before he went looking for fruit on it?

Did Jesus not say that he brought war not peace, how very calm and pacifist was the Jesus presented in of Luke 12? If, Peter did slice off the ear of one of those who came to arrest, Jesus did he do it totally without command from his commander? When you read back, you find that Jesus had told them to sell their garments and buy swords and that one sword was not enough. In the Shemitic traditions, it is believed that whatever takes away the outer cloak of a Man must be a very serious debt, not to mention the garment. Even Moses advised them to show mercy to debtors by not taking even their cloak, but here, Jesus told them to sell their garment and buy sword, who has no sword. So, for Jesus to have acquiesced and calmed down, may just be to Fulfill all Righteousness and draw more Souls in; and more to that, TO SHOW THE POWER OF RESSURECTION. Again, did Jesus not whip them in the Temple, over turning their tables? When they advised him not to go to Jerusalem that the ground was flaming in stalk of him; what did he say? He said ''Go tell that fox ...'' and who did he call fox?

Was Jesus without Nationalism? Did he not say that: ''I am not sent, but to the lost Tribe of the house of Jacob''? What about Jesus show of Nationalism? Did Jesus not tell the Gentile Phoenician Woman that: ''Do not cast the Children's bread to dogs'' , ...and the Woman begged for the crumbs as dogs do? How did Jesus speak to his Parents when they came looking for him? Scriptural Pundits have wondered that after that incidence, Joseph, the Strong, was never mentioned again in the New Testament.

While Jesus is the Son of God and the Most Holy person to have ever lived, and Worshipped, he did not put his Disciples and Apostles to such enslaving, rigid, crude, self-denying, torturous, self immolating, maladjustive, maladaptive, exploitative, etc., life style that some congregation put their adherents in order to enslave them. Jesus and his Disciples and Apostles were not dressed in their time as the typical Shemites dressed, they may have dresses like Roman Socialites, and Mary Magdalene was dressed like a ''Free Woman.''

Harvest is for only those who had planted or sown, therefore, harvest, which is the reward part of the work, investment or sowing, and where harvest is also the heavenly part for those who help themselves by sowing, cannot be possible on Earth, unless One had first Sown Seeds and cultivated and nurtured it till harvest's time.

Patience is only for those who have sown, invested, worked, traded, invented, acted, created, constructed, etc. To have patience, when One had not planted or sown is not patience.

ASSIGNMENT

To achieve the desired and proper ''kingdom life'', the Edenic Life of Prosperity, a Man has to sow it and toil patiently till it is time of fruition. Man, by planting, can manifest the ''kingdom life of heaven'', when he finally harvest what he has sown.

To know that prosperity on Earth goes to the Practical Planters. He who plants, will reap. He who saves his money, over time, will have a principal or capital to invest or acquire assets. He who put his money to work, will make profit, so that, more in turn is added to him.

If, One has not planted, his patience is useless and a waste of time because he will have nothing to harvest for his acclaimed patience. To have or discover something to sell is also a way of planting and when the profits come, he will have that as harvest, as those who have will thrust in their sickle and reap for they have patiently toiled, worked, from the time it was planted, till now that it is ripen to reap the harvest.

All those who say that they are patiently ''waiting for God'' to do it for them, when what they are actually waiting on God for, is their acute responsibilities and duties, and who have not planted anything, spiritually or physically, wait patiently for what night and day?

Patience is the [Process Time], between planting and harvesting. One must have been engaged in a solution oriented task for him to say that he is patient. Also, to be busy without doing something productive, and just with folded arms in empty waiting, while expecting, is not what is called patience in this parlance, but an act of the slothful. A person must be able to differentiate between the Waiting and Patience. A person may wait with a waiter attending to him, in that case, he is being served and he will pay. A person who is Patient is the person who is engaged in a Solution Oriented Scheme and is Processing Something, so, he is a processor in a processing time; but a lot of people who call themselves Patient People, are just in Empty Waiting, they have not attendants they are waiting on, nor are they attending to themselves, nor are they in a processing time, nor are they engaged in any solution oriented task. The only thing about them is that they are suffering from promisism, faithism, hopism, expectationism.

One has to wake up and find something to plant and cultivate, and God Almighty will give the increase to support his mustard seed effort, so as to harvest prosperity.

From the parables of the kingdom, it is clear that only those who can achieve a Life of Divine Wisdom from

God Almighty, will make a good living for themselves, by working at it. Philippians 4:7-8; Proverbs 13:4;   Proverbs 19:15.

Q

HIDDEN TREASURE AND PEARL OF GREAT VALUE

Matthew 13:44-47

Men sought for hidden treasure and the pearl of great value

NUGGET LINE:

''The kingdom of heaven is like a treasure hidden in a field which when a man found it, he hid it again and then, in his joy, went and sold all he had and bought that field''

NUGGET LINE:

''In his Joy, he went and sold everything he had and bought it...When he had found one of great value, he went away and sold everything he had and bought it.''

INFERENCE

What is the Kingdom of God? What is the reality of Heaven on Earth? What is the reality of Heaven on Earth as it is to be manifested? What is the Household of God? Ephesians 2:19; Romans 8:17. What is the Kingdom Life? What is the Kingdom Prosperity on Earth? What is the Will of God Most High on Earth?

If the ''Kingdom Life'', lived here on Earth, does not bring in/on even a semblance of the KINGDOM BLESSEDNESS, what value has it then, and on what basis and use is its claim?

Is it not the Work of Christ (Word plus Spirit of God Most High), on Earth, to manifest the Kingdom Life on Earth? And of the Kingdom Life on Earth — and would not the Kingdom Life on Earth be as Edenic, paradisiac, if, Salvation is wrought as it should be from the beginning? Is not therefore, the Kingdom of God Most High (Glory to Him), also here on Earth?

Is not prosperity —all round prosperity, the hallmark of the realization of the Kingdom of God Almighty (Most High) on Earthy? —When it begins to be ''achieved'' and ''constructed to be'' on Earth as it is in Heaven?

What is it then, is meant as: ''To be on Earth as it is in Heaven'', if it does not become Heavenly on Earth? And if it be on Earth, as it is in Heaven, would not

then, the Earth be Edenic, Paradisaic?
Matthew 6:10.

''Your Kingdom come, Your Will be DONE ON Earth, AS IT IS IN Heaven''.

The ultimate plan of Salvation, is to return the Earth to its Original Purpose, and to its Edenic and Paradisaic glory and Worship of God Most High, as it was from the beginning.

The Hidden Treasure and Pearl of Great Value, is the Word (Logos) and the Spirit (Rhema) of God Most High (Blessed be He). And the Word and Spirit, is the manifestation of Divine Wisdom and Spiritual Intelligence, of God Most High.

The Word and Spirit, being Christ, is the ''Divine Inspiration Testimony'', which Testimony is the Rock, which Rock is the Foundation, which Foundation is that on which the Edenic Kingdom Life is built; and which is to come, and which could be now and also forever. The body of the people who bear this Testimony, is the Kingdom Livers of the Elohimic Realm.

Therefore, Divine Wisdom is the authentic Foundation. Check Divine Wisdom as the Hidden Treasure and Pearl of Great Value, in the Scriptural book of Proverbs 8:1-36; 9:1-6. The Divine Wisdom, which is the without-which-not , can only be found in those who are imbued with, and bear within them the Word and Spirit of God Most High (Most Holy), which bestow on them, the gift/spirit of Revelation and Prophecy and Knowledge, and making the operate with the Excellent Spirit. And they radiate and vibrate with/in the Aura and Essence of God Almighty, even so.

The Word and Spirit Anointing, imbued on the One called, as the Fruit of Everlasting Life, which is the Scroll, of which Prophet Ezekiel said: ''Thy Word was found and I did eat it''; which is the White Pebble of Knowledge of Life and Living, of which is spoken of the Scriptural book of Revelation; it that which gives the beingess of Being, the elixir of Life, attunement ot the Deific Order, , as of the Melchizedek Priesthood Order, from the very Realm of the Elohims (Creative Spirit Energies), by which to make your sphere or space Edenic, Paradisaic, Heavenly, which is the Kingdom Life, even while the New Earth has not yet come, as WILLED by God Most High (Benedictions to his Name).

Therefore, having found that Logos and Rhema, which is the Hidden Treasure and Pearl of Great Value, a Man goes out selling all that he has had to HAVE the money to BUY IT, and lo, even so was it said of the Kingdom Life, of the Kingdom of God on Earth TO BE AT HAND, that is, has already come to those who can have this Revelation to REACH FORTH AND GRASP IT, and even to grasp it by ''force'', for ''the Kingdom of God suffereth violence''. Although, this does not mean indiscriminate target aggression, stealing, etc., but, that the Kingdom Life, leading to The BLESSEDNESS, of which prosperity of the Kingdom Life is included, is for those who STRIVE TO ACQUIRE FOR THEMSELVES THE KNOWLEDGE OF IT. STRIVING is the Violence of it, because the Evil Cohorts will do everything to keep a person from it, to such extent as using mind thwarting, mind locking, mind blocking, spiritual disorder, poverty, etc.

It is the Bread and Wine of Divine Wisdom, as mentioned in Proverbs 9:5; which is the Wisdom of The Excellent Spirit, given to those who earnestly strive to get it, as mentioned in James 1:5.

Therefore, hear this very well, Jesus said: ''Eat my Flesh, drink my Blood'', then, he represented and presented The Flesh as The Bread, and The Blood as The Wine, in the Lord's Supper or Holy Communion.   Also, in Proverbs 9:5, we are told similar thing, that the Bread and the Wine is the gift and present symbolizing Divine Wisdom, to those who have the grace to hear and heed and understand the call of Divine Wisdom, that, such are the Ones invited to the Banquet of Wisdom or Wisdom's Banquet.

Therefore, know this, the spiritual symbolism of the Lord's Supper, Sacrament or Holy Communion, unknown to many people, is to represent and to pass, bestow, give, show or imbue with THE DIVINE WISDOM and SPIRITUAL INTELLIGENCE, which only God Most High gives to those who ask it of Him. James 1:5.

Therefore, the Holy Communion was to OPEN THE EYES, of the called Ones to receive the Divine Wisdom, and the secret Spiritual Intelligence, with the Kingdom Life of Paradise, of which the Earth is to be made to be like in the Will of God Almighty, so that, while others merely take the Holy Communion as a ritual or feast, some are chosen to have the Divine Wisdom and Spiritual Intelligence, as the Pearl of great value and Hidden Treasure; only God Almighty gives it, and to only those who deserve it; that is, who ATTUNE Themselves, to the AURA and ESSENCE of God Most High, Jehovah (Benedictions to His Holy Name), to have it. Proverbs 8: 22-31.

When Jesus, after his Resurrection visited them, they could not know nor know him, but, when he took bread and broke it and gave it to them, together with wine, as the Sacrament or Holy Communion, their eyes became open, and they became privy and complicit to the hidden understanding and knowledge, and they, then ''knew'' and ''knew him.''

So it is, in the advanced revelation, of which This Daniel prophesied, that: ''Knowledge shall increase.'' The Word + The Spirit = Christ = Divine Wisdom. And this Wisdom is said to have been with God Most High (Blessed be He), from the very foundation of the World and beginning. Proverbs 8:22-38; and which Wisdom was at God's Right Hand, in doing, making, creating all things and from which all things were made, and which Wisdom is the Word and Spirit that hovered above the Water and the Waters, and which Wisdom, is also defined as God. Check Proverbs 8:22; John 1:1; Genesis 1:1;

Genesis 1:2;   Revelation 1:2;
Isaiah 55:1;   Revelation 22:17.

Divine Wisdom calls: Come to the Waters and drink freely of the Water of Life. The Water of Life is being symbolized here also as the Wisdom that gives Everlasting Life, which Everlasting Life, is the Resurrection Life. Amos 5:24; 5:8; John 3:5.

The Blessedness of Paradise, which is symbolic of the Kingdom of Heaven on Earth,, which is made manifest by the Kingdom Life of those Attuned to the Aura and Essence of God Almighty, to have Spiritual Intelligence of the Excellent Spirit of Divine Wisdom, after having the Word and Spirit imbued on them. It is available even now. One can now know that the Word is the Spirit of God Almighty, which is Divine Wisdom.

Yes, total paradise has not yet come, but the BLESSEDNESS of God Almighty in Paradise, has begun and abound, even now, in this very Life on Earth, by the possession of the Pearl of great value and he Hidden Treasure, as given to those who know, to those to whom it is given, and of such blessedness of paradise, evidenced by THE JOY, rapturous Joy. They feel the prosperity of The Joy, thereof, which prosperity is different, because it abides within the VINE, as having that Communion with the Realm of God Most High.

Therefore, things work differently for different people, in different places, differently, and for different reasons, based upon their Attunement and Connection to the Divine Aura and Essence of God Most High, because they have the information and knowledge.

To abide as the Branches, to the Strong Vine, which Vine is the Divine Wisdom, coming directly from God Almighty and leading back again to Him, as He, God Almighty is The Infinite Life Source.

It is the ''Blessedness of Paradise'', which has come to this Dispensation, that is being thus given, preparatory to the Full Coming of Paradise; and those who bear or have ''The Knowledge of the Testimony'' wrought by The Word and Spirit of God Most High, do get, do get The Blessedness, which has the sign of immense, inexplicable Joy, hence, giving green light to the coming of the ''True Riches'', of which it is spoken of as, the reward for those who had been faithful in small things or talent they had had; and attendant to it are healing, redemption, salvation, deliverance, transformation,

prosperity, transubstantiation, revelation,
inspiration* etc.

*''And, He shall write His
Word, in their Hearts'' Joel
2:25-29.

R

ALLUSION OF THE PARABLE IN
THE NT., TO THE PROVERBS IN THE OT.

Parable is an allegorical representation or story of something in Life, which carries a meaning for necessary adjustment to Life and Living. So, a parable may be fictional or is just fictional, after all, but with the intent to pass a message, physical lessons, moral and spiritual codes, an experience or an information.

A Proverb is a popular story, which may have come from history, legend, story, facts, theories, experience, conventional wisdom, etc., and may appear as a maxim, by-word, statement, quote, utterance, adage, dark sayings, riddles, enigmas, etc., which informs about a particular knowledge, truism or experience.

Therefore, parables and proverbs are made, to give Practical Lessons, in making an Excellent Living, physically, spiritually and otherwise.

The Parables of the New Testament alludes to the Proverbs of the Old Testament, manifesting the Epiphany*

*Once again, remember that, in relation to The Pearl of great value and the Hidden Treasure, The Epiphany is the Celebration of Divine Wisdom, for, Divine Wisdom is the Pearl and Treasure.

1

      Wisdom as Bride or Bridegroom who invites to the Banquet of Wisdom: Proverbs 20:22; Matthew 25:14; Proverbs 9:5;   Proverbs 13:9, and as related to the Ten Virgins.

2

      Wisdom as the Diligence that brings Prosperity: Matthew 25:14-30; Proverbs 10:4; Proverbs 13:4;   Proverbs 20:29; Proverbs 18:16, as may be related to the Talent.

3

      Wisdom as the ''Rod'' of Correction to bring Discipline: Proverbs 13:24; Proverbs 14:12; Proverbs 5:20; Proverbs 18:6; Proverbs 21:17; Proverbs 21:20; Luke 15:12; Proverbs 27:11; Proverbs 3:11; as may be related to the Prodigal Son.

4

      Wisdom as The Foundation with/on which to build all things, big or small, plenty or few, physical and spiritual. Matthew 7:24-27; Luke 6: 42-49; Proverbs 8: 22-31; as may be related to The Wise and Foolish Builders.

5

Wisdom as the Shrewdness of the Wise Manager. Proverbs 22: 3; Luke 16:1-8; Proverbs 21:30; Proverbs 9:16; as may be related to the Shrewd Manager.

6

Wisdom as a Mustard Seed with which to start anything, not despising the days of little beginnings: Matthew 13:31-32; Proverbs 6:6-11; Proverbs 30:24-28, as may be related to the Mustard Seed.

7

Wisdom as the ''Watchfulness'' (or defence, insurance, security, savings, investment, trade, preparedness, vigilance, charity, carefulness, business principal, etc.), as may be related to Watchful Service. Luke 12:42-48; Proverbs 31:1-3; Proverbs 28:20.

8

Wisdom as a Thing that brings Reward, interest, earning or payment, whether spiritual or physical: Matthew 20:1-5; Proverb 4:10-17; Proverbs 10:13; Proverbs 14:24; as may be related to Workers in the Vineyard.

9

Wisdom as the Harvest for the Wise who had planted and cultivated what was planted to reach fruition. Mark 4:26-29; Proverbs 10:6; Proverbs 10:16; Proverbs 15:19; Proverbs 19:24; Proverbs 20:24; as may be related to Sowing Seed.

10

Wisdom as a Hidden Treasure and Pearl of great value: Matthew 13:44-47; Proverbs 20:7; Proverbs 1:1-6; Proverbs 8:12-21.

The Worthy Epitome, of all these is: ...Let us hear the conclusion of the whole matter, Worship God Most High (Glory to His Name), the Creator and Maker of All Things... Ecclesiastes 12:13-14.

This means that, all along, from the very beginning (or Genesis), to the End, yet to come, DIVINE WISDOM is the only key, and it the Nugget for Prosperity and Victory in Life, and the epitome of all, is to WORSHIP GOD ALMIGHTY, yet, this means ONLY Worship of God Almighty NOT religion nor self-righteousness.

So, what are the Scriptural parables and proverbs saying? They are just saying: Get WISDOM and WORSHIP God Almighty.

S

SYMBOLIC CONNOTATIONS OF THE PARABLES.

The Presentation of the Scriptures, is in material and physical form, that is, your Scripture is hardware, hardcopy, solid material/matter, because Man is in the Physical, mundane , material World of Matter, although, Man has a Spiritual Origin too.

That which ignores the Material-Physical Welfare Concern of Mankind on Earth, is swindling and destructive and can not serve Man a dot.

Come to think of it, the parables are Fiction Stories, told with Physical-Material Characters and Elements, connoting physical and material meanings and relevance. The Physical State of Being and Beingness, manifests the Spiritual.

On this case of the Balance needed for the Spiritual and Physical Life, there are lots of analysis. It is believed, in some quarters that the Parables of Jesus, like the Ecclesiastes of Solomon were uttered towards the end of Jesus' Life on Earth, just as the Ecclesiastes were written towards the end of Solomon's Life on Earth; hence, not without Experiential Thesis, which the Proponents of Jesus' Divinity and Deification as God Almighty, may have attempted to cover, in order to make him seem without Human Nature, and free from any form of frailties or foibles, commonly associated with Human Nature. Although, no matter how genuine their attempt of deifying and equaling Jesus with God Almighty, might have been, Jesus' show of hunger, thirst, etc., may have shown that he was not without Humanity or fleshly cravings.

The Experiential Thesis in the Parables and Ecclesiastes is made more factual and supported, by Jesus' seeming comparisons of himself and Solomon, especially, when he had said that: ''A Wiser than Solomon is here'', of which Pundits analyzed that, he was actually referring to the Physical and Spiritual Balance of his Parables, as compared to the Proverbs and Ecclesiastes of Solomon, of which some of them opinionated that Solomon may not have revealed; yet, some assert that he may have also revealed that in/through the Temple's Construction, which serves for Spirituality, by/for Worshipping God Almighty in the Holy Temple. With this, it is surmised that, while Jesus may have made more Vocal Effectuation and Miracles of the Spiritual Aspects of things, as in bringing a Balance between the Physical and Spiritual, Solomon, by building and constructing the Holy Temple, also revealed Spiritual Balance and that the Holy Temple he built was a Miracle too.

Whether the Pundits are right or not about Jesus and Solomon, the SPIRITUAL BALANCE ought to be attained by everyone, and that we are placed in a greater advantage TO LEARN FROM THEM THE LESSONS, just as St. Paul alluded to that they were given as examples to us, and Jesus, himself said that ''Greater things than these shall ye do'', showing succinctly, that Jesus may not have seen himself as the limit, and there was still room for improvements and development leading to ''greater things than these.''

The Physical-Material, comes before and precedes the Spiritual for the Earthling or One Living on Earth, a fact hidden from many people by exploitative religionism and spiritism.   1 Corinthians 15:46;   Psalm 30: 9.

The highest and best Spiritual Activity is to Worship* God Almighty and Organize Call to Worship of God Almighty, after that Worship, ALL other things done, is mere ritualism show and ceremony for sectism, congregationalism, religionism, etc. Even for a Priest or Clergy, his Work is NOT any other thing but, to Organize Worship Mass. It is for the Call to Worship and Organization of the Worship Session or Mass that the Priest is recommended for Ecclesiastical Benefice, but not for religion, spiritualism, nor ritualism.

*The Highest Spiritual Activity is described as [Session or Mass of Worship of God Almighty], against the misconception that the highest form of Spiritual Activity is that which deals with fasting, ritual sacrifices, self-flagellation asceticism or other such complexity

The poor in spirit and others who have spiritual dependency and despondency may think that Spiritual Ascent and Prowess and height are attained by such self-immolating activities, sacrifices, rituals, etc. are wont to want to measure Spirituality by the extent of such things as self-immolation, sacrifices or ritual, and with that misapplication and misunderstanding, they are held in thralldom, expending themselves and their wealth.

The highest Spiritual Activity is Worship of God Almighty, and as the seeming simplicity of it may not satiate those who may wish to draw advantage therefrom for themselves, they have concocted and made Spiritual Ascent to look so difficult, complex, harsh, hard, immolating, expensive, etc., that the People always stand in need of Spiritual Middle Men, before they can attain Spiritual Ascent.

The Way to God is simple and express Way through Worship, not needing any Middle Man or Third Party. It is only in the quest for Knowledge, that One may then need guidance.

The two-edged ''Sword'', works for the spiritual and physical. Therefore, the relevance of Spirituality, for the Earthling or Human Being, involves the significant interaction with Nature, hence, with Matter; that is, the physical and material.

God Almighty is manifested in the existent Created Things. He is the God and Maker of Matter, hence a Materialistic God of the World of Matter. God Almighty is Felt in existent creation, just as the Wind is Felt, but not seen. The regularity and order of the Rising Sun every day, proves Creation's Design by a scientific God, for verily, The Sun, shows in it operation, the Scientific Method.

God Almighty can be seen, if only One could see through the Sun, through the FireLight that enwraps Him. Psalm 104:2. It is intellectual shame to assert that, only that which is visible to the open eyes exists, that God Almighty does not exist just because one can not see HIM. Does a Man see the Air he breathes? So, God Almighty stands with the material, tangible and physical, stands with Matter. For, He (Most Holy), made a Material World of Matter, for significant reasons.

People who treat with levity, and disregard, the Physical Earth Life, either for religious utopia or fools' paradise or misapplied heaven-gaze, or anything, are against Divine Will of the Creator. Can One expect reward from the Creator after abusing, destroying, vandalizing, spoiling, etc., God's Creation?

Even Jesus, himself, had to make use of Material Symbolism, else there will be no way for him to reach out to that which exists clearly in the physical, as Man is. Man came from the primordial, pre-mundane Spiritual Matter, to grapple with Earth-Matter, the physical, material, tangible, solid, etc., so as to prepare him for the Yonder Material Exegesis of finer Post-Matter, which shows vividly that, Man is materially engrossed, whether on Earth or after the Earth, because, Spirit, is also Matter, that is, ethereal Matter. Here on Earth or after the Earth Life, Man has no escape from Matter. Man is Materialistic by Nature, and any pretense about this, leads t severe imbalance and evil.

Man must therefore strive in constructive and productive Work on Earth, to strive and thrive to make his Earth Life meaningful, happy, prosperous and with liberty. One may not have to waste a second, with religionists who say that: ''Your Spiritual Welfare is our concern'', because, he would not, in the end, be able to take care of the ''spiritual concern'' that he is so much smug about, having despised the very person/personage that contains the spirit or is the container of the spirit; he does not care about One's Life a dot. One must give such a very, very long distance and gap; for, such may end up putting

One's mind, body and spirit to thralldom. For disregarding the physical needs of his members, and holding it with levity as trifle, worldly, carnal, etc., himself, ought not demand any physical work, sustenance, material or money, from the very people he boldly says to that he has no concern for their material needs, but, only concern for their spiritual needs, showing himself clearly to any serious thinker, that he presents ''a cake not turned'', and therefore, is bizarre. Even if a preacher may not be able to give material things to his followers, he could still preach about self-development.

TABLE 1:

SHOWING THE CONNOTAION OF THE
PARABLES IN PHYSICAL AND SPIRITUAL
INFERENCES.

    The numbers that are written from
one to ten, on the left margin, shows and
represent the parables and the order of
the Parables, as they appear on the
Content of this book.

PHYSICAL	SPIRITUAL
1. Material things by which to thrive.	Spiritual gifts and fruits of righteousness to use to worship God Almighty.
2. Material preparation, as a type of personal insurance preparation and security and defence against lack or sudden needs	Spiritual Light (Logos) with which to seek the Most High God
3. Financial, material and structural accountability, property rights, responsibility, profit, making, practical wisdom in/on duties and obligations for Excellent Living and Living Standard. And	Honesty in service and worship of God Almighty.

never forgetting that, nobody may help you with your own responsibilities.	
4. To avoid life of profligacy, prodigality, wastefulness, emptiness, void, darkness, poverty, improvidence, lack of basic needs and general lack.	Call to repentance , forgiveness, contrition, penitence, penance, restitution, to Offended Man and God Almighty.
5. Proficiency, expertise, skills, know-how, diligence, etc. and just about all that a person can do with training and learning to prosper in/on his job or trade.	Commit you service of God Almighty and Worship of God Almighty to God Almighty.
6. The resources one has in hand, or what is available to him without any other choice, is sufficient to start mobilization for any project, venture, business, trade, etc.	Have faith and hope in God Almighty.

7.

One has to stay very competitive, and learn everything he can learn to defend his trade, project or business. And One has to know that Vigilance is the only Guarantee, not holiness, nor religiosity nor any other thing. Once he losses Vigilance, he is on zero.

Watch for the day of God's promise and/or visitation.

8

One must adopt best practice and practice, stay efficient, be ten times better, keep to oaths of allegiance, organization ethics, laws, etc. And one must be very diligent to prosper on the job, by having something to fall back on when the job suddenly ends, either as a virtual insurance, such as intellectual or ideal property and right; or he could have relations or relationship to money, such as family. One must have security of basic needs, if not, he does not exist, at all. And such basic needs must not be company's properties, because company will evict him once they disengage him.

Faithful service to God Almighty.

9.

One must Invest   as a
first law to fight poverty
and make a pension for
himself to escape and
avoided the much
dreaded old age
suffering, which people
without any pension
arrangements suffer.
One must know that he
is getting older by day,
and may not be able to
continue to work as he
is doing now, which is a
fact. God will give
strength, but a Man not
propertied is in throes,
and Asset Properties are
the best boon. Never
wait to be told.

One could do
Evangelism.

10.

One must know this,
that without Practical
Wisdom, as relates to
meeting needs and
challenges promptly,
negotiating his way
through, arising to the
demands of Life and
Living and occasions of
his life, he is nowhere,
nobody and does not
exist

One may need
the Anointing.

T

THE PLACE OF CHARITY OF THE PROSPEROUS.

One may never have known that, if, at all, any body needs Prosperity and Wealth most, it should be the Righteous and Worshipper of God Almighty, who needs the Physical Properties, Logistics and Structures, to Secure himself physically and spiritually, as he is often persecuted, stalked to be harmed, abused, bullied, hated, witch-hunted, etc.

It has been studied that it is the poor, but righteous worshippers of God, that are the most frequently persecuted, and from this study, it has also been observed that once they get into a measure of Wealth, and acquire Needed Securities, especially, of the Basic Needs, the persecutions stop totally or abate; and also, that many of them change their Belief Systems or Life

Styles too, when they get into the money.

Therefore, some pundits assert that, the Attitudinal Change that occurred when they get more Financially Secured, is the strongest factor to ending the persecutions; while that may be true, it is known that quite a lot of poor or Less Secured People are persecuted worst and often, because of their stupidities, and not necessarily because of their religious bigotry. When they change to constructive-

thinking-life-style,
the persecutions
abate or may
reduce a bit.

The Righteous
need The Securities
which a measure of
Material Wealth
can provide, to
Secure his Basic
and Living Needs,
in order to avoid
destructive
compromises,
abuses, and the
entanglements of
some such rash
oaths/vows,
imprecations,
maledictions that
may come from
eating the ''bread
of sorrow'', due to
lack.

The practice
and application of
Faith is Industry,
that is, Constructive

Industriousness =
Habitual Diligence
= Work = Faith.
James 2:14-20.

   The relevance of
''Faith with Works'',
which St. James
spoke of/about,
has to do with
MATERIAL CARE in
relation to CHARITY,
which extends to
meeting Living
Needs, and that is
Charity of
economic and
industrial
significance, even
though some
religious zealots
and bigots, who
are so smug of their
so-called ''your-
spiritual-welfare-is-
our-concern'',
while totally
ignoring the
Material and

Physical Needs of their adherents, fail to admit the fact of Charity, being based on Matter/Material, and can not be effectuated without Material Structural Giving. And this is more appalling when One considers that, the preachers were not even expected to give such material gifts to their adherent, but ought to teach Sound Principles that will allow their adherents to Prosper so as to be Secured in their Basic Needs, and avoid slavery, apostasy, servitude, thralldom, cultism, spiritism, etc., that

lack of Basic Needs
may cause; but,
they seem rather,
to do worse, by
setting dogmas
that rather
impoverishes their
adherents the
more, than they
were, and
subsequently
making them to
beg food from
misanthropes,
spiritistics, cultists,
and malevolent
people or be
enslaved for food,
which is horrible.

It has been observed strictly that the concept of ''Materialism'', as is being propounded by some religious sects, may not actually exist, and that, if, at all it exists, could only apply to the super-super-wealthy tycoons or moguls. This is made more factual when One observes the average GDP or GNP which the populace live in, battling with the insatiability of human wants and the increasing Consumerism.

This brings on the question that how could they ever commit the so-called sin of ''Materialism'', even if they have wanted to, considering the increasing Consumerism? This is why the Pundits and Analysts, surmise that, when the ratio of Consumerism is made with Materialism, the adherents in the Congregation can not afford Materialism, even if they had wanted to, due to the economic purchasing power, as relates to consumerism; meaning that, in a life time, most of them may not even be able to own more than quadruples of any particular commodity, and if they can not be able to acquire quadruples of anything they need, how can they be described as tending towards Materialism? Also, it is agreed that there are inheritors, beggars, disabled, dependents, etc., to consume all the Material, meaning that when the burden of leaving inheritance to Children or Offsprings, giving alms to the needy, and taking care of disables and dependents are added to it, what then is left of to make them seem tending towards Materialism? Therefore, it is weighed that the proponents of Materialism as a sin in the Congregations, may be out of the mark, and that Materialism does not exist, other than as a preachment icon to make preachers look good in their self-admiration.

There are people who think that the Work-of-Faith, is merely and just about religious ritualism, dogmatism, self-flagellation, fasting, etc., contrary to such people and contradicting them, correctly, when St. James, gave example of what the Work-of-Faith is, he referred clearly and succinctly to PROVIDING FOR THE MATERIAL AND PHYSICAL NEEDS OF THE BRETHREN OR PERSON. James 2:15. That, further certifies that, the Work-of-Faith is not religiosity, but actual Physical Charity- and Charity requires Industry to come about, even while Worshipping God Almighty (Benedictions to Him), which extends to the fact that, Prosperity without associative industry, creativity, works, art, etc., to meet the actual Human Needs and Demands, and the subsequent maintenance of life, towards a better Living Standard, is not prosperity. Prosperity has to give back to society, because people have a Living to make, even as they Worship God Almighty.

Furthermore, in the Revelation of the ''Last Day Judgment'', in the Parable of the ''Goat and Sheep'', Charity is DEPICTED CLEARLY AND SUCCINCTLY AS THE ONLY CRITERION AND REQUIREMENT, by which to be vindicated, exonerated, saved, and upon which to enter the Kingdom of Heaven and the Paradise. Matthew 25:31-46.

Take note that they were not asked about their religious bigotry. CHARITY TO MANKIND, was just the only certificate and testimonial to enter be accepted by God Almighty.   Proverbs 11:23-26; Luke 3:10-11.

One can not evaluate nor do Charity without economics and industry, in the practical and material sense of it, which covers all field of Human Activity. One can see that Jesus did not include Religious Activism, as the basis for justification. Just as St. Paul spoke of,

''Though I speak with the tongues of Men and of Angels, but have not Charity, I am nothing''   1 Corinthians 13. Why?

     The whole Law and Prophets, the whole Scriptures, hinge on Charity- and the implicate and explicate rendition of Charity, is the GOLDEN RULE – ''Do to Men, as you would have them do you''- and by that, you summarize the entire Holy Writ or Bible, into a single Sentence, ''Do to Men, as you would have them do to you'' and it is also true as ''Do to Men as they do to you'', in adjudicating, all because you know Human Needs, and can in your own small way, help as far as you can.

          A poor Person, can not do Charity, and any form of prosperity which can not give back to Society, is just vain hedonism, narcissism. Prosperity without industrial application does not promote the GDP or GNP, nor improve the means of exchange, hence, uneconomical. The prosperity of a developed people could not have not come about without labour and industrial activities. Prosperity does not mean that everybody becomes zillionaires, nor involve in vanities, after all, everyone can not be zillionaires; yet, a Society can still be said to be developed and prosperous, even when every one is not a zillionaire. Therefore, integral m prosperity, is about the individual development that accumulates to collective development, which is all about progress from stage to stage, and about Advancing Living Standard, and being Well-To-Do. And in fact, it the well-to-do People, that form the bulk of the industrial machine that move the Nation forward, and it the well-to-do People that really have the actual wealth.

U

INVOCATION FOR DIVINE PROVIDENCE AND FORTUNE

Spiritual ''Awakefulness'', is to know the hour of God's Visitation, and to be Vigilant and Self-Reliant, to resist the Evil-Covetous Ones who perpetually bring UNPLEASANTNESS.

DIVINE PROVIDENCE, is God's Visitation per time, because Zion, is Divine Providence per time: It is spectacular for some time, which means that, it is happening for only when God Almighty Wills/Choses to send It. The Miracle of Divine Providence comes on its own particular time, unsought for most of the time, and although, Man may pray to request for it, Man can not requisition it on demand as, if, it is his wage or salary package which he had laboured to earn nor can he commandeer God for it, as, if, God is his messenger. For, God Almighty is not his robot.

If, One gets It after Prayer, it means that he is highly favoured, because, One can also get it even without Praying at all, most people got/get it without Praying at all; It just comes on and off like Luck, because God knows even before One asks. Prayer and Righteousness are no conditions for Divine Providence, which is why Prayer and Righteousness helps to give One MORE LEVERAGE ADVANTAGES to be ten times better, when he adds it up to the general Divine Providence

God Almighty does not sleep nor slumber. The divine Providence, comes like a Mustard Seed Opportunity, and that is why, only those who are grateful and know value, and can make profitable USE of small things, can get It.

St. Mary, the Mother of Jesus, was like a distant protégé of Prophetess Hannah, the Mother of Samuel, and that is evidenced, when you compare the Songs of Hannah with the Song of Mary. 1 Samuel 2:1-10;   Luke 1:46-55. And both Songs/Prayers/Chants, echo in the Song of Moses. They were all Psalmists as well. And chanted and prayed the Psalms always. For example, some of the Psalms that Jesus frequently chanted sang and prayed, are: Psalms 113; 114; 115; 116; 117; 118; also, as revealed in Mark 14:26.

Jesus sang and chanted the Psalms before he died for the Sound Power of Resurrection. There are Psalms for chanting, which bring Divine Providence (or commonly called Zion) and Fortune. Some of these Psalms are given here, but the exclusive treatment of them, is in another book by the Author.

Some of the Psalms for Divine Providence and Fortune, include (but, not limited to) : Psalm 92; 118; 24; 94; 100. (Note that One could chant the Psalms into Water, Oil, Balm, Ointment, etc., for use). Also, Psalm 1; 20; 19, for Divine Inspiration. Chanting these Psalms must be preceded by Psalm 51; 100; 150; and ended with Psalms 150 and 100. Psalm 27, must be chanted morning and evening. Psalm 27 is for all round Divine Protection and Spiritual Intelligence, Vigilance and Self-Reliance. Psalm 99 is for Divine Presence and Attunement to the highly needed Aura and Essence of God Most High (Great Glory to Him, Most Holy Jah, YHWH)

These Invocative chanting Psalms, do not take away self-exertion and work towards practical problem-solving, rather, enhances it; nor does chanting the Psalms, replace sound medical treatment and consultation. This is because, chanting the Psalms bring Divine Presence, hence bringing Elohimic Angels (Working Angels) to One, so that, they will boost One's Work and give the Increase, meaning One will receive less or nothing when not connected with Work in the line of his Prayer Request. That is why One could observe that some people tend to do ten people's Work and stand ten times better, than all others around him, because of the Elohims working with him. A lazy person may not invoke the Elohims, because he may harm himself thereby, as they are the Creative Spirits of the

''Let-Us-Make'', who are the ''Elohim-Us-gods'', They Work with Workers or Doers.

The Supernatural and Divine Providence, are not in the whim of Man to control, Never mind those who say that they do control the supernatural and

Divine Providence, they merely say that to entice or swindle. Divine Providence is a Cosmic (Heavenly) Smile to garnish One's own individual and personal efforts to work for a quantum leap advantage or leverage, with the help of the Elohims sent by God Most High to One's aid.

Divine Providence does not take away personal calculating responsibilities and work, it is a handsome additive to One's toil to give One the leap, flight, leverage, edge etc., which makes One to be ten times better. Divine Providence and Miracles are garnishing or additives to One's toil and labour, it is what is called: ''God gives the Increase'', or in popular African terminology, it is like what is called ''Jara'', giving to a customer or hard worker as a bonus.

PROJECT

FAITH ISSUES VERSUS WORSHIP OF GOD
ALMIGHTY

    Contrary to deceptions, God Almighty does not need Man's Faith nor Beliefs to be God or do His Things or perform miracles. Love, even causes much healing and/or miracle than Faith, but this Love should not be misinterpreted as ''Laying down your One's Life'', for, One has got to Live, while Loving.

    Faith, big or small is not the cause of miracles. Faith may have just been used by as an apology or excuse by religionists to massage their egos, protect their stomach, defend their ministry or pretend to defend God, when a miracle did not happen. They may think that the people will leave their congregation and hold them and their ministry as untrue when an expected miracle failed, and so, they tell the worshippers or congregants that it is their lack of faith that caused the miracle not to have happened; and this cowardice to brace up to the truism of failed miracles, is a major problem in religionism. They failed to let the people know that God may not answer all prayers and that when a miracle did not happen, it just did not happen. What is the point of accusing the congregants of their lack of faith as reason for failed miracles? Would she have come, if she did not believe? Imagine the accusation of lack of faith over the decades on sincere worshippers who have come all the way to worship God, and sustain the clergy and the congregation using the spiritual and physical resources, and One can just know how far the preachers can go to cover a lie. Do they read Jesus at all? Jesus said a Faith as tiny as a Mustard Seed, can move mountains, and if that be the case, is the Faith that moved a Woman from her home, paid the fares, paid the offerings, paid the tithes, sweep the congregation, pray for the congregation, fast for the congregation, donate for the congregation, advertise for the congregation, evangelize for the congregation, etc. and etc. not more than a Mustard Seed? If a tiny Mustard Seed Faith can move mountain, does this Woman, with all she has concentrated on, not have even a Faith as the size of a Mustard Seed to have solved her problem which is not even up to the size of a small broken boulder from the mountain. If a Faith, tiny as a Mustard Seed can move a Mountain, why are these problems not even up to the size of a coconut not yet solved by prayers in the ministry?

Check and see, the toughest, grandest, greatest miracles happened in the Exodus, where the people did NOT have Faith at all, not even up to a fraction of Mustard Seed, nor did they believe a dot. Even their leader doubted, for which he was given several signs; and yet, God kept DOING.

Worship of God Almighty does not depend on supernatural miracles nor on faith and beliefs; only the poor in spirit and the indolent sloth worships God Almighty for miracles or supernatural things.

Worship of God Almighty is a compulsory, regular and MANDATORY DUTY, for the GIFT OF LIFE and LIVING, which is above all supernatural miracle claims. Check what King Solomon said in Ecclesiastes, which may have been written at his old age, he said: ''Hear the conclusion of the whole matter: WORSHIP GOD, for this is MAN'S DUTY ON EARTH'', miracle or no miracle.

If the person's Life that comes through Procreation and Birth, does not give the person enough Awe and Gratefulness to Worship God Almighty, with personal freewill volition without coercion or sermon, then, NOTHING else under the azure plane of the expanse and firmament will make him Worship God Almighty with Joy and Gladness of Heart.

God Almighty does His Things or Miracles or sends Divine Providence TO GLORIFY HIS NAME, and for SPECIFIC PURPOSES, therefore, whether a Man Believes or not, have Faith or not, He remains I AM THAT I AM, and the Sun will still rise, the Night will come, Nature will remain, and He will remain God Almighty.

''God is not a Son of Man, that He should repent.''

One can then see why and how a lot of so-called Faiths and Beliefs, apart from being used as spiritistic deception machination and impeding progress, self-awareness and knowledge, are mere Presumptions. The Presumption of Faith that takes them to the precariousness of even daring in commandeering God. And, he, in the grandiosity of his presumptions which he calls faith, does not reflect on the absurdity and obscenity of having a Mighty God, which he mal-uses.

Imagine such grandiose presumption, to dictate to God, his God, and that the actions, doings, movements, operation, etc., of God, should be based on his so-called faith. What is his size in comparison to the great creature of creation, is he bigger than Behemoth, Leviathan, Dinosaur, etc. which God had hidden in the Deep, just to allow Man to thrive? Job 38; 39; 40; 41.

If ten Leviathan or Behemoths, whose skins have tough immunity to resist any ballistic missile, be released to the Earth, to walk the Orb, can the whole population of Man defy them?

And the Psalmist cried: ''Who is Man that Thou, O Mighty God visiteth him?

When/if the parlance of Faith and Belief thought and held by the many are peeled off, shattered and blown away, only then, can a whole lot of people receive illumination, redemption and salvation, because the so-called Faith and Belief, had been the intoxication, the ''rose coloured glasses'', the ''ivory tower'', opium, the deception, seduction, malaise, disorder, etc., that had KEPT THEM BOUND IN THRALDOM.

Every now and then, Human Children, begin their babyhood, by being immersed and soaked into Faithism and Believism, which becomes a Strong Net, in which they are encased for the remainder of their Lives, subjected to the buffeting, immolation, flagellation, torture, etc., through DOGMAS of spiritism and religionism, unless they BECOME FORTUNATE to have that Strong Net of Faithism and Believism broken and torn, and only by such breaking, can they, now FEEL the fresh air, and first handedly, begin to EXPERIENCE NATURE, and subsequently FIND GOD HIMSELF, and SEEING HIS GRANDEUR FEELINGLY as never before, STOOP TO WORSHIP HIM, without any coercion or dagmatized preachments of Believism and Faithism, that had hitherto, BLOCKED AND LOCKED HIS INTELLECTUAL MIND, from EXPERIENCING GOD PERSONALLY, that had been hidden from them, by the ''Jezebel'' called Faithism and Believism.

Our Parents do not give us everything, yet, they remain our Parents; but God Almighty gave us everything needed to Live in Nature, and even gave much more in advance, hidden in Nature and Earth, which those who explore, keep discovering every day; except the Management of them which is OUR RESPONSIBILITIES. Is it then, not absurd that, One fails to see all these, and cry the cries of sloths accusing God or denying him for not ''breastfeeding'' them, on top of all these?

Therefore, Man's problems are Man's faults, not God's, because, Man was given freewill volition. Man was not made a robot, he is responsible and accountable for his Earth. There can be no Paradise or Heaven for the Earthling Man, until he makes his Earth such Paradise or Heaven, the more he delays to transform the Earth, the longer he Lives in the throes and woes he has put himself in. After Man has succeeded to Edenize the Earth to its Paradisaic format, he will then be given the Knowledge to discover the Fruit of Life in Nature to Live for ever, which hitherto, had been hidden in the Deep* (*: the deep that calleth unto deep''), away from him, because there was no need for him to Live forever in an Earth not yet made Paradise by Man. Even Paradise is Man's duty to make.

There can be no favour without labour, for, even religious congregation houses could not have been built without the gold or money earned from labour. And, that is why Charity is the highest –and the Kingdom of God is likened unto Charity; and Charity is the ONLY Work of the Kingdom of God Almighty. Charity to Mankind.

When a Man says that he is like God, more-like-God than-others, or even claim to be God, in his faintest presumptuous Faith, how then, can God show him and teach him and reveal Wisdom to him? Therefore, the chief cause of the problems in the Lives of many people is their Faith and Belief. This is different from the healthy belief in One's strength and skills to solve problems. James 1:5. As far as they have boasted to be like God, God leaves them, after all, God does not need God!

Does a Man really know. Who is it who knows in a multiple variances, what will exactly, will happen next year. We plan, prepare, equip because we know not what may befall. A simpleton calls his presumption faith.

ONLY GOD ALMIGHTY KNOWS.

V

WORSHIPPING GOD WITH JOY AND GLADNESS OF HEART

''Beloved, I pray that you may prosper in all things, and be in health, even as your soul prospers'' 3 John 3.

There is a high benefit and significance in worshipping God Almighty with JOY and GLADNESS of Heart, and making Feasts and Celebrating with People. No One who is prosperous becomes that without spiritual intelligence, even though he may not be Born Again, meaning that, the Born Again, which some Congregation presents may not lead to Spiritual Order, and that there are some people who are not in Church or not called Born Again, but who have higher spiritual intelligence, and even spiritual superiority, perhaps, because of their striving for The Peace and Justice in their democratic or liberty quest for a better World Order, and these global Peace Mission of theirs, seeking for the tranquil Universal Peoplehood, may have brought them to become imbued with the AURA and Essence of God Almighty. Yet, in spite of all these gigantic Missions for The Peace, Liberty and Justice, etc., some people do not affirm their mission nor regard them as doing God's Work, simply because they do not think of them as ''born again'', in their dogmatic sense of it; but, remember that Jesus did say that: ''Blessed are the PEACEMAKERS for they shall be called Sons of God.''

Quite a lot of time, religionists have allowed their dogmatic alignment to refrain them from the true path of Humanity and Humane considerations, especially, as regards concepts in their religious dogmas that define what

''Service to God'' really is, when such concept as ''being born again'' is considered. Could One serve God, without first serving Humanity or Man tangibly and physically? Could One offend God, who had not offended Man? Is not service to God, in the end, service to Humanity or Man? And One may ask, should a service-to-God always be without benefit to Mankind and be only in HOPE and expectation for the beyond? Therefore, pundits have wondered why people who have actually not done any viable, constructive, inventive, physical or tangible thing for Humanity, but have led millions to their deaths, and put other large numbers of such, in maladaptation, servitude, maladjustment, immolation, flagellation, etc., in the name of Faith or Belief, receive such affirmation or eulogies, as the greatest of Men that ever lived, while neglecting the PEACEMAKERS, who Jesus rightly referred to as the Sons of God. While some may claim that the Men of Hope did give their Souls to God, on which account they are thus worshipped, One wonders how can Man give to God, what God has? And have the physical work of others not in any effort synchronized with service to God? Should not Man be asking Soul or Life from God, instead of giving Soul and Life to God?

Before Jesus called the Constructive and Peace People to be Sons of God, did he not see the Religionists, who in their wanton self-admiration in their Work of Hopism, would gladly, nay longingly wished to be called ''Sons of God?''; but Jesus by-passed them, looked the other way and called the constructive and peace people as the blessed sons of God. Jesus could have known, that the Earth could not have been stayed without them, and that if everyone went the pharisaical way, the Earth will become extinct.

Even so, we hear: ''He causes the rain to fall on the religious and non-religious'', therefore, it is surmised that, the difference is just in who has greater spiritual intelligence, as such will be the one with spiritual superiority, to make THE

BEST USE OF THAT THAT IS, and God calls them HIS People, as in Laudate Dominium, (Psalm 117), even when religions regard them as non-conformist, non-initiated, or non-born again; for, they may not even understand what Jesus meant by being BORN OF THE SPIRIT.

The Concept that Jesus was teaching, was:

Born (brought forth) of/from [THE SPIRIT], which is just about DIVINE ATTUNEMENT, but not the religious born-againisn, being held by proselytizers, to initiate people into their sects through dogmatism. Jesus was not winning people to any sect or congregation, as do holders of bornagainism do today, in which once a person leaves their sect or congregation, he is termed as backslidden and no more bornagain. The question is: Why should the leaving of a person from a sect or congregation, connotes his leaving God, whereat, God is omnipresent?

From this we can see that those Prophets and other Worshippers of God, who predated Jesus' coming had no need of bornagain, but had need of being [Brought forth from The Spirit], showing that, Divine Attunement was Jesus' focus by that. This complies with the assertion that, while some people had not been or are not in religion, they were/are being used also used by God, and vindicated by Him, especially for their constructive projects and peace making missions to Humanity or Mankind. Such people, although, not making presumptuous claims to Faith, Belief, Bornagain, have been called Men of God, by the World, even before the Christian era, by study of such historic names as Zeus*

                    *: Zeus may mean
            Son or Men of God or
            gods).

Jesus announcement, declaration and statement of Peacemakers as Sons of God, which include Global Peace Missions against terrorism, slavery, abuses of Human Rights, oppression, etc. could never be taken as a mere abstract statement that has nothing to this Earth and Earth Life, hence the utilitarian scope of the greatest happiness, liberty and peace for all, who make proper use of, according to the original purpose of, and AVOID ABUSES. It is desired for spiritual power to develop and improve the physical life, and if not, what use has it? Until the greatest number are happy, democracy is not working.

A person with spiritual disorder and malaise; paranoia, with sever spiritual lows, manic depression and dejection, or who has no spark of Spirit, may not prosper, and he can not worship God with joy and gladness of heart.

Merely being Born Again, without being ''Brought Forth From THE SPIRIT'', has no DIVINE ATTUNEMENT and/or Alignment with the Aura and Essence of God Almighty; therefore, can not accord Spiritual Intelligence, and spiritual superiority to rise above the Cohorts of Evil physically and spiritually. Matthew 5:20; Proverbs 4:7; Proverbs 7:22.

The word: ''Rich'' is extensive in meaning, therefore, application of being well-to-do to ''Rich, as in bringing in creativity, better living standard, industry, construction, development, inventiveness, etc., has to be added to it to make it prosperity. This means that there is Richness that may not be prosperous, where it lacks industry. Prosperity is not vain utopic idealism nor slothful expectationism, hopism, etc., of which Talents are hid, buried or locked-up. Deuteronomy 10:21;   3 John 3; Deuteronomy 8:18.

The focus of   Econo-Industrial Theology,   is to make people to be physically and spiritually well-to-do.*

*well-to-do,

as a better

application

word than 'rich'.

and having intellectual- intelligence and vigilance-plus,   and   good   health, because, God gives them the power, which power, is the industry, skill, trade, talent, idea, creativity, health to earn wealth. And He sends His Word plus Spirit to them through revelation, inspiration, idea, etc., with which to be ten times better in all aspect, and have a Life of Balance* and Excellent Living. Deuteronomy 8:18.

> *The extensive meaning of Evil is Imbalance as ''not balanced'', which then causes Covetousness in the One who is not Balanced.

There is NEED FOR BALANCE in all things. There is no Evil, but Imbalance. To ignore BALANCE, leads to, indifference, offences, hurt, abuses, swindling, mesmerism, bad seduction, manipulation, deceit, spiritism, negligence, (even criminal negligence), etc. God Almighty does not want his people to be like that, or be imbalanced. God Almighty saw that ALL that He made was BALANCED, by the existent Creation Laws. No mesmerism.

BALANCE IS WHAT GOODNESS IS. We may not be Perfect, but, when we strive towards achieving BALANCE in all that we do, we invariably aspire to GOODNESS, which Goodness is DOING RIGHT THINGS, and thereby, come into the Field of Perfection.

It is said that: ''Ephraim is like a cake not turned'', meaning that, people who offer to Men, Righteousness, but, deny them Prosperity only make them Slaves to All Things, physically and spiritually, in the end, and worse, make them unable to Worship God Almighty with JOY and GLADNESS of Heart. It is the place where they used dogma to cause imbalance in their adherent, that ,makes them exploit the adherents, and when One check the sects and their dogmas, One finds so many imbalances set by the founders, unknown to the adherents, wherewith, he swindles them.

Somebody who does not worship God Almighty with Spiritual Intelligence, is like a spiritual orphan lost in the jungle of wild beasts, left bare to the mayhem of spiritistics.

Why should One have righteousness and go to slave for Demons and the Ungodly, for bread? Perhaps, the notion and dogma of keeping the Righteous Poor, in the guise that poverty is pleasing to God Almighty, is the stupidest dogma from Hell. Is the One who can not provide for his household not regarded as an Infidel in the Epistles? How can he provide being Poor but Righteous, without money or relation to money, and without trade, industry, creativity, investment, art, construction, etc.

Then, the Demons and Devils are happy that the people are kept poor, hence, unable to fulfill their responsibilities. How can the One who is righteous, without currencies fulfill his obligations and responsibilities promptly?

Apostle John, who was even closest to Jesus, gave a BALANCED CONCEPT, with Balanced Priorities in   3 John 3. He gave the injunction first for the prosperity of the physical and health, then followed by the spiritual. The physical needs are prior.

When ever religionismic people put dogma to cause Imbalance, there is a whim to mesmerize and delude people, nay, exploit, swindle and take undue advantage of them.

 There must be BALANCE, between the physical and the so-called spiritual welfare, so that, people CAN WORSHIP GOD ALMIGHTY WITH JOY AND GLADNESS OF HEART, because, there are severe causes too ill to mention here for refusing to Worship God Almighty with Joy and Gladness of Heart. Deuteronomy 28:47.

How can One be only interested in spiritual welfare? Where is the Balance? Will the One minister to ghosts congregation? Is God Almighty (Glory to His Name), a sadistic Monster and Vampire who takes pleasure and delight in peoples' afflictions, persecutions, suffering, poverty, wretchedness, etc. Psalm 30:9

Is it not some people's stupidities that put them into persecution and poverty, even when their paranoia, hysteria, spiritual malaise, presumption, etc., make them think that they are suffering for God and giving God their Lives? Ask: What are they suffering for God Almighty and why? Is the Life they boast of giving to God Almighty not God's? Who gave them the Life in the first place? Should they not be giving to God Almighty the Praise and Benedictions due Him for the Gift of Life, and asking God Almighty for Life instead of wasting their Lives in religiosity and saying that they are giving God Almighty their Lives by that? God Almighty gave them LIFE as a Gift. Moses said: ''Choose Life, that ye may Live''

''I worship God'', seems to be more relevant and useful than, ''I trust God'' Why? God may not need One's Trustism, for, most times, and many times more, people who boast of Trusting God and Divine Destiny, do, in the end come to apostasy or put the blame on God, or even deny Him, thereafter, after perceived seeming failure in answers to their prayers; when actually, they were the Ones that failed in their duties, obligation, responsibilities or have been slothful. God Almighty demands One's Worship as a duty, not Trust, after all, He is beyond One's Humanity to do ''business'' with.

People who boast of trusting God, may be full of presumption, and may even co-equal themselves with God, but, God is not any One's business Mate or Colleague. JUST WORSHIP GOD, whether the situation is good or not; for, we are all indebted to him, for the Gift of Life.

The law gives Grace and Liberty; and gives the window or door for escape, expiation, penance, restitution etc. There is no grace and liberty outside the Law. Morality is the cloak of the Law, and morality also comes from the Law.

One problem is that of the misconception or misunderstanding of the ''Christian Liberty'', which seems to promote antinomianism and lawlessness. There would have been no need to start looking for Liberty from the Dogmatism they had sunk themselves into, if they had first of all stuck with the Civil or State Law. The Systems of Beliefs, commonly called religions, depend on the Political State for their Security and Defence, for which One is made to wonder why they did not simply stick to the State or Civil Laws from the beginning, instead of forming and following dogmas or doctrines.

Can a Religion not exist which follows the State or Civil Laws and makes no Laws of its own?

The Ten Commandments and other statutes, laws and by-laws which are in the Shemitic Scriptures, are in other words, the Constitution and State or Civil Laws of the Shemites, with their Traditions, as One may realize that Moses was involved as well, in a Nationalist Movement and was raising an infantile Nation, for which he was Governing. Understanding of this will lead the Systems of Belief in various Places to honourably abide by the State or Civil Laws and Constitution of the Land they live in, as far as it does not command them to commit manslaughter or other evils. Romans13.

Then, people can just go into their Congregation, and organize Worship of God Almighty and leave the Laws to Government, and have nothing more than Ethics of their Systems of Beliefs.

The foundational, fundamental, basic, core and primary Duty of the Priest, is just for Worship*

   *Call to Worship and
   Organize Worship of God
   Almighty,

   But, NOT to form Dogmas.

Pundits have surmised that problems started when religions made themselves adjudicative structures in place of Governments. Moses could say: ''Eye for Eye'', because Moses was King of, and represented the Government he was forming for the New Nation he was building. Quite a lot of people think that Moses' Laws are a kind of Religious Laws, but they are wrong. In spite of the fact that Moses seemed to advocate Theocracy, he was The President and Aaron was the Chief and High Priest, so that whatever Moses did was Governments Action, so, it was Government giving the Ten Commandment and saying: ''Tooth for Tooth'', as a Civil Law Justice System. Moses held the dual mandate, of KING-PRIEST, as of Melchizedek, so also, Samuel, Daniel, Nehemiah, etc. Quite alright, God called Moses for which he doubled as a Prophet, while Presiding, as Chief Commander of the New Nation emerging. And quite alright, God gave him the Laws to make a People, rather than Beasts.

Antinomianism and the often drummed Christian's quest for Liberty, makes One to wonder and ask:

''Who had bound them?''

So, One can see that they had erroneously exchanged Dogmas for Laws. And when Dogmas begin to suffocate and immolate them, they come about screaming for L-I-B-E-R-T-Y!

If they had just stood with the State's Civil Laws and Constitution from the beginning and held unto the good traditions of their Ancestors, they would not have come out seeking a ''liberty'' from ''law''. How can one dare attempt to go lawless? Where two or more people meet law becomes mandatory, because of need for agreements, oaths of allegiance, terms and condition etc., and where there is no law, the place becomes a Jungle of Beasts.

When some Christians tell themselves that they are free from The Laws, or Moses' Laws or Laws of Old Testament, One can just pity them, especially when they use ''Grace'' as excuse.

Really, what they want freedom from is the crude dogmas and doctrines of their sect, NOT Law; because One can not in his right mind, wish for a lawless state. Note that Psalm 119, is the longest Psalm, and it EXTOLS THE LAW and speaks of ''LOVING THE LAW''. So, as long as PSALM 119 is, so is the long arm of the law.

Now, what laws are they free from? Will they watch them go in into other people's wives and leave them? Will they allow them steal and leave them? Is it freedom to commit crime?

When people talk of freedom/ liberty from the Law, One can just pity them for the torments of religious dogmas they have been ensnared in.

One's Government never calls him a criminal till he is tried and found guilty, and he is weighed on the Balance of the Law, if, guilty he pays for the charges, and after that, he is free before God and Man, but the dogmas that the Christians follow, seems to have consigned them to condemnation in ABYSS and HELL, even before they sinned?

Dogma is NOT Law. Dogma kills, the Law bring Justice and the Peace which gives Life. Many Christians, fail to differentiate between Law and Dogma, and Live all their miserable Lives in the HELL which their religion have put them, and no wonder they are always crying for L-i-b-e-r-t-y, Deliverance, Salvation, etc. And an outside onlooker, just wonders why a Human Being made Free by State and God, Lives in thralldom, and the onlooker does not even see him as bound, not knowing the severe Spiritual Malaise and Disorder those Christians Live in.

They go loose claiming to be Free from the Law. What kind of stupid Liberty is that? If he thinks that he is really free from the laws of Moses, which is The Constitution and Civil or State and Government Law, but which he never knew, or deceived about by Misapplied Grace, let him go to the open Market and try to steal some commodities, then we shall know whether he is really free from any kind of laws. Even God, Himself, is not ''Free'' from the Cosmic Laws and Laws of Creation fixed by Him. The Sun obeys the Cosmic Laws, and has never failed in a demi-hemi-semi fraction of a second ever since the Earth was made, MYA (Millions Years Ago); thus we have Sunrise and Sunset every day. If the Sun ever fails to obey the Cosmic Laws for a single day, the Earth may become extinct.

So, he thinks he is free from the Law, and that is why he loves Christianity and Jesus so much, swept away by Lovism, Pharisaicism, hopism, etc. Which law is he free from? Who will carry his cross for him? Who answers for and is accountable when he offends? Has he ever seen Jesus materializes from nowhere and say: ''Hey, punish me, not him''? That Jesus died as a sacrifice for sin, is just the same way we have democratic martyrs, abolitionists, freedom fighters, etc. One is only ''Freed'' in the Soul.

Therefore, be wise as David, and never fall into the hands of any Man, if not, tough shit. The fear of the harm that People can cause, is the center of Wisdom.

To confirm this, hear St. Paul, who One may have claimed to be champion of the so-called ''Christian Liberty from the LAW''

''EVERY MAN MUST WORK OUT HIS OWN SALVATION''

St. Paul.

Will a Person go on causing mayhem and hurting People and be spared, because of his claim of Christian Liberty that has freed and exempted him from the Law and its Penalties? Could he marry a Wife, without a Law? And for the One who marries is his Wife's Father, not called   Father-in-Law''

Come to think of it, if at all, One is to gain Legal Immunity over Penalty, Litigation or indictment, is it not the Law that gives it, and is that not Grace? How then can a People claim to have attained Exemption from any Law Old or New without existing emanant and imminent Law granting such Immunity or Exemption?

Therefore, even the Grace or Liberty they speak of is GIVEN BY THE VERY LAW. Where is Defence without law, especially for the fatherless, orphan, helpless, disabled, widow, poor, handicap, etc.? Can Humans exist without Laws?

It had been tested and tried, that even Liberty can not be managed without Law, and even in a place where all laws were scrapped, laws still existed.

[This was done in a homestead where all the people decided to abolish all types of laws for a year. Do you know what happened? It was not just possible, and at the end led to war, after sometime, when the vindictiveness borne burst. Mr. A. did not want his locker opened when he was not around;... Mr. C. wanted lights off by ten pm;... Miss B. rather preferred not to have anyone touch any of her things without her giving it;...And so on. It was not up to three months when they decided to make some laws for themselves.]

Barbarism, injustice, dishonesty, racialism, jungle, misanthropy, malevolence, etc., are what comes without law.

Democratic Government is set to represent God to bring Justice, Liberty, Grace, Forgiveness, Happiness and Peace for All.

One can not simply say that the Law should cease, simply because he feels that the Law is inhibiting him from some perceived pleasures, which is the angle a lot of Christians are taking at it.

[They felt that the Law was restricting their quest for pleasure, and so relinquish and abolished it, thinking that, absence of such Law will bring Liberty and began to indulge in hedonism.]

The so called hedonism, which they then engaged in, thinking it was the Law that had been keeping them from it, was not even defined in a Civil Law as a Crime. Only their Sectist Dogma did. This then, clarify the issue that many are bound in the fetters of religionism from LIVING NATURALLY RIGHT AS HUMAN BEINGS AS ORDAINED BY GOD. And that is where all the cries of redemption salvation, liberty etc., are coming from. The truth is that, without the law, Liberty can not even stay; in all these, the conception is that, it was not even the Law that stole his pleasure or happiness, but Crude DOGMA, put by desperate Bigots, Zealots or Fanatics, who they have subjected themselves to, in the Sect or Congregation, they have taken themselves to exploit them. Only dogma steals One's Private Liberty, not Law.

[After they removed all Laws, to become free, they find that, they had by that, become worse than a slave.]

Freedom can never be got by the removal of all Laws, and this too has been tested. One may try it out and see, whether such Liberty he gets by abolishing all Laws, was not Hell.

It has then, been found, that they ensnared themselves to religious dogmas, that now puts them in thralldom, because of ignorance and cowardice, So, the Coward, thinks that, it is the Law that inhibits his pleasure and fun, not knowing that it his ignorance and cowardice. Try it and see.

Laws alternates Laws to cause motion and flight, and this is a knowledge that the captive to religion does not know, that in order to fly, he has to alternate the Laws, because there may be another Law against flight.

[So, what happened when they got the Laws removed? It was found that they were the first to cry out and lament, and more so, because the ''survival of the fittest'' which had been stopped by the Law and had preserved some, form the hell, was removed and they met face to face their waterloo, when the savages, cannibals, misanthropes, terrorists, barbarians, etc., came in; because the very second that Lawless came in, . Civilization went out and away.]

The problem is not Law, but DOGMA spun by religionism, it is the DOGMA that wear them the sacks, instead of comfortable clothes, not Law.

[They had been campaigning against the Law in their religion, and had abolished the Law, till the horror came, and being that they had never Advocated the Law, they could not Appeal to the Law for their Defence, which the Law would gladly have, even unto making a tunnel or window of escape for them; and being so repellent to the Law as they were, they met first hand, the very Lawless Vampires from hell, sent to pounce on them, and then, they wished, they had stood with the Law]

One could see clearly that cowardice and ignorance contribute to the concept of the abolition and relinquishing of the Law by those who seek that. What can the weak, timid, defenceless, coward, etc., People do in a LAWLESS JUNGLE OF CANNIBALS AND BEASTS?, ...And the stupefaction that the very weak, who ought to campaign in support of/for the Law, so as to cover, insure or camouflage himself there in, are the very Ones calling for the END OF LAW. How can he get his Rights without the Law?

For they had thought that once the Law is gone, they can do as they please, but they had forgotten, that while they thought that they could do as they pleased, other barbarians, brutes, cannibals, etc., could also do worse, and the very coward that cried against the Law and abolished it, can not now face the Lawless vampires, malevolent, terrorists, misanthropes, etc., that has now besieged them nor could he invoke the very Law that they had impugned. Why, now in the torment of real LAWLESS BEASTS, they could not meet their supposed Lawless MATCH.

''Be wary what you wish for'' is a popular quote, for One could have it brought face to face to him, what he had wished for, and he may not then, be able to withstand the very LAWLESS VAMPIRES FROM HELL HE HAD CONJURED UP NOR LIVE IN THE LAWLESS REGIME WHICH THE BEASTS NOW INSTALL.

It is in this light, that it is shown that the One who wishes to have a Victorious Life, must know how to keep himself with the LAW. Romans 13.

THEREFORE, One must SHUN DOGMA! Shun Dogma, even from a very far distance before it reaches One. AND ABIDE WITH THE LAW, and most importantly, knowing how to invoke the LAW and use the LAW, to secure One's self.

W

HINT

X

EPILOGUE

Industry is Creative Habitual Diligence in any form of activity that support making a Living, Meeting Needs and Demands of Living, and is tangible, feasible, artful, creative, constructive, material, natural, practical and of economic relevance as it constructively furthers creation.

Y

POST FACE

The Divine or Deific Fiat will rule The Minds of Men, and that, Men, will, by response to the Divine Fiat, rehabilitate, transubstantiate, transmute, transform, The Earth to its originally intended Edenic Purpose.

And Good will and Charity to All Mankind.

Happiness!

Liberty!

Z

Glossary

      This is a Glossary of Words with contextual terminologies as used in this book, though the etymological rendition and/or root may be same original, the syntax application may have been extended or rendered in ways to suit the peculiar diction usage as rendered in the book.

Holyism:

Useless ritualistic, feigned and insipid form of piety with Spiritual Disorder and without associative Charity, nor Constructiveness for self-development and better Living.

Religionism:

As used in this book, does not refere to any formal or structural religion or religious setting, but to inimical, inhumane, destructive, etc., Belief System and Dogmatism.

Religiosity:

Same as Religionism.

Pharisaicism:

Same as Religionism.

Expectationism:

Inopportune expectation of things not personally and practically worked for and with no cordial relationship to; or, of budgeting in such expectations, which are not feasible, example: One expecting his rent to be magically or miraculously paid, when he had not planned and worked well in advance for it.

Hopism:

Same as Expectationism.

Faithism:

Same as Expectationism.

Lovism:

Relying on love to solve physical problems, which are One's personal responsibilities, when he ought to have been calculating, planning, working, investing, etc., creatively, to solve it. Or the act of taking undue advantage of Peoples Love harm or swindle them. Or the act of making One's self, become prey to others, because he loves them without vigilance, watchfulness, intelligence, etc.

Trustism:

Same as Lovism, Believism.

Paranormalism:

Illogical and impractical dependence on the supernatural , mystical or spiritistic, when One had failed to do his personal assignments or home-work. Or fail to do all it takes, within Natural Human Efforts, as personal responsibilities demand. Supernatural or Mystical Incidence, happen to those who have done All that they could honestly do within Human Abilities, as regards the problems, before the Divine Intervention.

Spiritual Power:

Mind Power and acute intelligence, security, liberty...

Dependence:

This refers to ignoring One's Thinking and Faculty Powers, and the neglect of Self-reliance, jus because of religionism or to have the help of others or parasite others, for which there should have been no need, if, he had thought and planned right and had worked at it diligently and with more foresight. Here it involves both Spiritual Dependency where People are called to religion minus or sans their Brain or Intellect; and Physical Dependency where People grovel, or put themselves in slavery for no good reason, other than, they were slothful.

Slothfulness:

This refers to Mental Laziness and Refusal to use physical, practical and material means, acumen, etc., to solve Problems rationally and with reasonable practicality, when the Person is Healthy and even has the Time and Resources at his disposal.

Spiritism:

Refers to inimical, misanthropic or inhumane spiritual activities, which also ignores the practical and physical aspects, when it should not have been so, and succumbing to destructive energies, that swings him or he swings.

Spiritualism:

Same as Spiritism.

Spirituality:

Good and Excellent Spiritual Activities, which is Constructive Physically, and Spiritually, all about Worshipping God Almighty. It involves doing One's physical work, trade, business, etc., with efficiency that brings productivity and profit. It refers to Constructive Energies Manifestation and the Ability ot Apply the Intellect to physical and practical Productive ends, enterprise, art, craft, trade, commerce, industry, science, technology, etc., to meet real Living Needs and solve Life's problems rationally, using high Spiritual Intelligence. It refers to the Powers of the Intellect, Faculty or the Psychomental Powers of The Intelligence, and being able to organize Worship of God Almighty, personally. Spirituality is manifested through the Intellect, which is further manifested through physical work, therefore, the most spiritual, is the most inductive and prophetic, hence, the most intellectual, for, the highest intellectual quotient is revelation, inspiration or inductive reasoning. Yet, religionism had tried to kill the Intellect and disavows the Intellect, as it seek to make people who they can ride on as mulls, brainwashed people who would not think.

Churchianism:

This refers to buildings or structures, where Dogmatism is held at the expense of the congregants or people, who they call flocks or sheep. Same as Religionism or Religiosity.

Promisism:

This refers to a situation where people prefer to follow fake, irrational, unfeasible, promises at the expense of what is real, give-able, physical, practical, rational, reasonable, etc., and worse, for them to believe that such connivance and complicity to unreality is God's Way,

God's Pleasure or that they are devoting themselves by accepting insignificant faith, that is just presumption, especially, the willingly bear false testimonies as sign of faith, or when such promises come with conditions that can never be met, even when the congregants or adherents think that they can meet the conditions. They only end up squandering and wasting their vital energies reserves to the sole benefits of those who beguile them.

ABOUT THE BOOK

This book is the Work of the newly discovered Field, of Econo-Industrial Theology, by the Socio-Theosophical Analyst Samuel Elaigwu, of far reaching Socio-Theosophical Research, into the new and expanding Econo-Industrial Theology, as the way forward into the coming Future Centuries, to avoid another cataclysmic dark age. This, as related to the ''Kingdom Life'' Well-to-do Principles, condensed in also, from the Holy Scriptures.

Econo-Industrial Application in Theology is highly needed now for the Future, else, inapplicable religionism/religiosity will stifle the striving of the many, who form the bulk of the hearers, adherents, masses, populace or congregants.

The increasing need for environment-and nature-adapted Youths, with hands-on industrial application, while worshipping God Almighty, has become so glaring to everyone in this era. No longer much room for slothful paranormal ''sky-gazers'' lost in spiritistic expectationism and spiritual disorder of the third kind, if at all they are still to hold their place in the coming Future Centuries.

Habitual Diligence in Making a worthy Living and Worshipping God Almighty simultaneaously!

A synopsis of Socio-Theosophical Analysis into the new and expanding Econo-Industrial Theology, as an advancement to curb another probable cataclysmic dark age, that may be engendered by supernaturalismic expectationism in religionism, in the near Future Centuries.

Thank You.

ABOUT THE AUTHOR

Akogwu Elaigwu, is the founder of Integrated Methodologies and The Salem Sanctum. He studied HII at Futurelearn, Buckinghamshire.